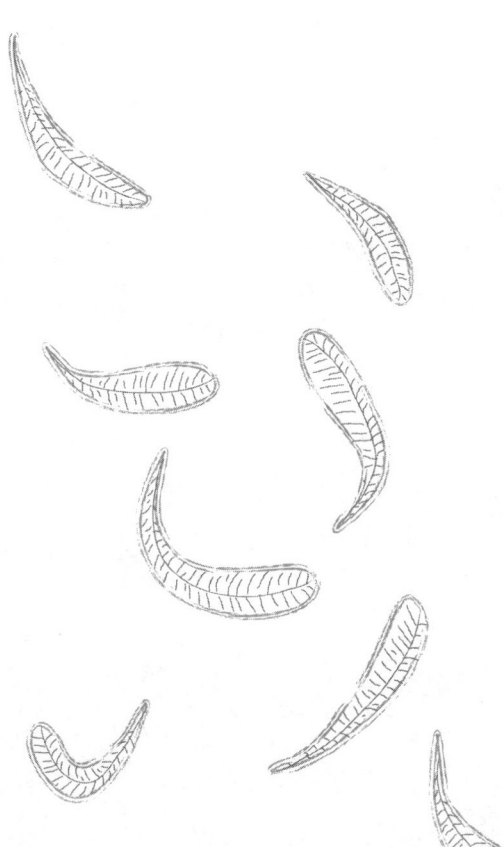

# Contents

## Part One

### Chapter 1

Feeling the presence of your guardian angel

### Chapter 2

Seeing the presence of your guardian angel

### Chapter 3

Hearing the messages of your guardian angel

### Chapter 4

Knowing the messages of your guardian angel

## Part Two

### Chapter 5

# Foreword

Discovering what you really want from life is not easy. I was lucky. I knew what I wanted to do from the age of fourteen – join the army and to be an Olympic champion. Didn't want much did I! I achieved both and often wonder how I made this happen. I have always been interested in success stories and how people manage to build something amazing from a simple beginning to reach their goals and dreams.

I am a fabulous dreamer! My greatest achievements in my life, however big and small began with a dream. I believe that success comes from taking our dreams and making them a reality. I do this by putting together a plan and finding the willpower to make it happen.

Though I achieved my dream of becoming an Olympic champion it didn't happen until I was 34! At times it wasn't an easy journey as some of you may know.

I will never forget hearing the words 'You've won!' I had won the 800m and then five nights later on the 25 August 2004 I won the 1500m. Two gold medals. This sort of thing usually only happens in dreams.

It hasn't just been my planning, willpower and dreams that have helped me. I felt guidance from another presence. I have always felt angels are around me and that they have helped me to stay positive and motivated. My angels have lifted me at my most difficult times.

In *I Talk to Angels* Beverley has put together a wonderful collection of ideas that will help you to find and connect with your angels. This is a book of inspiration, love and guidance which will help you be successful and happy in your life. It's a book that you can dip in and out of, to make notes, to plan, to dream and to make your own.

I wish you every success with your dreams, plans and goals, and remember, talk to your angels – they are always listening.

Dame Kelly Holmes, 2020

# How to use this book

> *"When your heart speaks, take good notes."*
> **Judith Campbell**

Dear Reader,

I have designed this book to be used by you throughout this journey as a journal for keeping your notes, doodles and everything else you share with your angels – your thoughts, hopes, plans and dreams.

There are plenty of exercises to help you along the way, including tips, activities and reminders as well as illustrations to colour in. There are also opportunities to jot down any actions or plans you wish to put into place.

I hope you enjoy using this book to journal and that you enjoy reading it, and learning how to talk to angels.

With love,

Beverley Densham

I trust my heart

I trust my heart and soul

I trust my intuition

I allow my heart to blossom and open like a flower

x

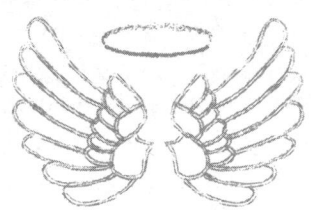

# Introduction

In this book I am going to teach you how to connect with your angels – especially your guardian angel

We all have a guardian angel, whether we believe it or not. Your guardian angel is your friend and your teacher and their love for you is unconditional. They are with you from the day you are born until you are ready to leave your body to enter a higher realm. They radiate so much love for you. I want you to be able to feel this love and I am going to show you how you can experience your guardian angel's light and the love they have for you and how they communicate with you.

I am also going teach you how to talk to your angels.

The presence of your guardian angel in your life is one of the most beautiful, celestial, angelic and incredible things that you can ever witness and experience. It can transform your life.

You really can experience a close relationship with your guardian angel, one where you receive unconditional love, where you can sense and feel the presence of your guardian angel. Most people think that this is something only a select few people can do. However, this is not true.

One of the biggest secrets of being able to connect to your guardian angel is to give yourself permission to get to know your guardian angel – and I'm going to show you how.

We have heard of people who are clairvoyant, and people who talk about seeing angels. You may think, "Well, I haven't, and I will never get to experience this." Here's the good news: you don't need to see angels to get to know your guardian angel. You can start by talking to them.

There are many ways to connect with your angels. One of the amazing things you can learn to do is to feel your guardian angel's presence. If you've picked up this book, you probably already feel that your guardian angel might be real and that you want to get to know your guardian angel. You know there is so much more to discover.

I know that your guardian angel probably led you to buy this book and read it!

Let's start at the very beginning. It may sound obvious, but the easiest way to communicate with your guardian angel is to do it every day – yes, every single day. Simply learn to incorporate it into your daily life from the moment you wake up in the morning. Making time to do this every day will, I promise, help you in every area of your life if you allow it to.

It may seem a bit strange to begin with but the key to being comfortable with this is practice.

Practice makes for improvement at anything and this is explained brilliantly in the book *Bounce: The Myth of Talent and the Power of Practice* by Matthew

Syed. He describes real-life examples and explains that many of the most well-known musicians and athletes did not achieve overnight success – they had to put in over 10,000 hours of practice. But not just that, they often had access to the best teachers and team members to help them too. Fundamentally, there needs to be a practice work ethic and the same applies with learning to communicate with your angels.

*"Do more than believe – practice."*
**William Arthur Ward**

The more time you spend developing your skills – and it can be simply reading this book and applying the tips, exercises, meditations and affirmations every day for the next 365 days – the more you will improve. You will learn to develop new skills and you will no doubt, I am sure, be able to communicate more clearly in your everyday life with your angels.

To begin with, communicating with your angels takes a bit of getting used to. You won't see or hear your guardian angel like you would your best friend. Learning to develop your communication skills means first recognising the subtle signs of your guardian angel reaching out to you. You will learn to develop your own unique relationship with your guardian angel. Although they may or may not seem visible, they can have a big impact in your life.

What a gift – to be able to have help in making wiser decisions, feeling happier, enjoying relationships more, and seeing your life, relationships and work flourish.

Our guardian angel communicates with us in a combination of ways and we can experience this in the following ways:

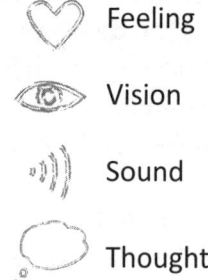

Feeling

Vision

Sound

Thought

This is also known as:

**Clairsentience** – feeling the presence of your guardian angel.

**Clairvoyance** – seeing the presence of your guardian angel.

**Clairaudience** – hearing the presence of your guardian angel.

**Claircognizance** – thinking and knowing the signs of your guardian angel's message.

In the first chapters you will learn how to connect with your guardian angel in all these four ways.

However, you will most probably find that one of these channels will be easier for you to connect with your guardian angel than the others. More often than not you will receive more than one sign and you will receive them through different channels.

For example, you may be out for a walk on a day you are not feeling so good and you see a little angel feather telling you all is well.

You could also, at the same time, hear a tune on the radio – or a song will pop into your head that will be relevant and helpful to how you are feeling.

Your angel will only show you a sign if it's positive or going to help you.

Whatever sort of day you are having, your angels are there for you. It may be that you are not feeling particularly good that day. Listen to your heart and soul. Listen to your body and emotions and look for signs from your guardian angel in the form of seeing, hearing, feeling and knowing. Be reassured. They are always there with you. They will be close to you. They will help you, guide you and comfort you. Be open to receiving their messages.

An angel prayer is a wonderful first step and a daily tool to help you receive your guardian angel's wisdom, guidance, help, and love for you every day. Make it a habit to say this prayer every morning.

# I Talk to Angels Prayer

*Guardian angel, please surround me with your unconditional love; shine your bright light on me for guidance, for positivity, healing, happiness and inspiration. Let your light shine on me like the sun, in my life and my work. Guardian angel, please help me to talk to you and to receive your guidance and love. With gratitude, I thank you.*

**TIP!**

**Write it out or copy it and stick it up on the wall for you to repeat and enjoy every day, especially first thing in the morning. You will be asked in this book to say this prayer quite often.**

Throughout this book I am going to teach you many ways of discovering and deepening your connection with your guardian angel. You will learn how to receive their guidance, unconditional love and support during the challenging times and the good times in your life. Feeling the presence of your guardian angel is such a wonderful thing. Learning how to increase your clairsentience is where we will begin.

This is the start of your journey. This space is for your notes. This space is for you to journal with your guardian angel.

**Journal with your guardian angel**

Write down whatever comes to you about the words you have read, the thoughts you have or the signs you are receiving, however small they are. They are guidance from your angels. This guidance you receive from your guardian angel will always be helpful, positive and healing for you.

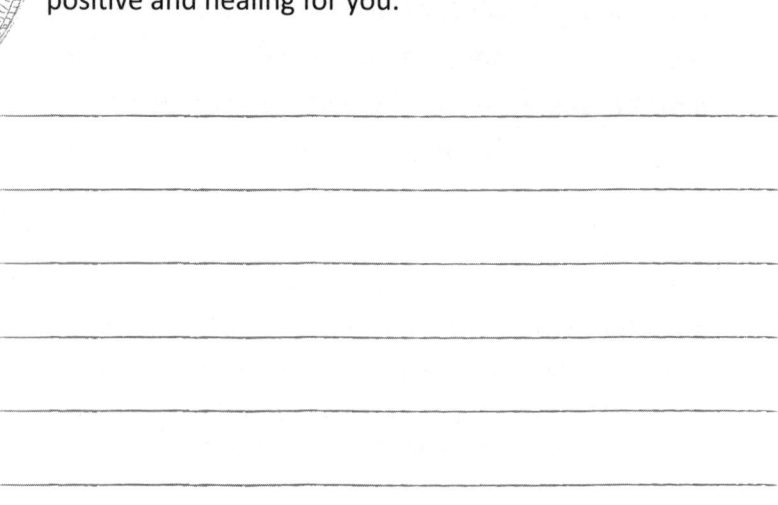

---

---

---

---

---

---

# I Talk to Angels Prayer

# PART ONE

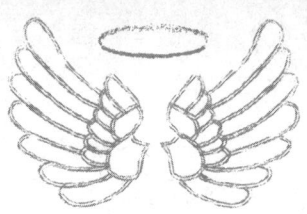

# Chapter 1

*"Angels only care about what you look like on the inside. A pure heart is the vessel that contains a soul's true beauty."*
**Molly Friedenfeld**

## Feeling the presence of your guardian angel – Clairsentience

Clairsentience is the name for feeling your guardian angel's presence.

The wonderful thing is that your guardian angel, if you give them permission, will show you their beautiful angelic wings of love, giving you angel hugs, and helping you feel their loving presence, especially during times when you need comfort, love and support. Or simply in your everyday life to help melt the stresses away and guide you to receive more happiness.

When you are feeling sad, you will feel their wings of love wrap around you. You will learn that you can have this feeling all the time. How wonderful is that?

When you need to make decisions, your guardian angel loves to help you have more clarity. I will teach you the tools to feel your guardian angel's presence so they can help you with decision making.

Angels love to point out good ideas too. You know the ones; the ideas where you haven't taken any action yet. Your guardian angel will give you angel nudges to prompt you. You may receive this angel guidance in the form of feeling angel tickles, angel goose bumps, or tickles at the top of your head, your nose or face. When something is a really good idea, you will feel this. It's their way of saying, 'Do it'.

Another way you can feel your guardian angel's presence – and it may not happen so often – is one of your ears may feel warm or hot. This can be your guardian angel getting you to take notice of something in your life that you are thinking or reading about at that moment. Or you could be in the middle of a conversation. If your ear gets very hot, it means that something is worth taking notice of.

**An exercise to strengthen your clairsentience**

Find a little white feather, although any feather will do, and run it gently over your face.
What do you feel?

---

This is what it feels like when your own guardian angel tickles your face.

They will do this to say hello to you, to make their presence known to you. It is their way of saying "You are not alone, you are safe, protected and loved and will be guided always on your path in life".

Your guardian angel will create angel tickles to show you their very real presence and to acknowledge they are with you, to send you love, healing or an awareness about a decision you are about to make. For example, you may be speaking with someone about a good idea that you have yet to act upon

Feeling a tickle is your angel's way of letting you know you should take action. They can also send subtle tickles that mean "Listen to me, I am your heavenly helper and I will keep you on the right path".

You may also feel a temperature change, or a sensation in a part of your body, perhaps on your ear, or a tickle on your nose, cheek or head, or over your legs and arms.

Take time to notice it, to feel it. Listen to the guidance you receive.

## Meditation

## What is Meditation?

Meditation is something that encourages relaxation and awareness, as well as focus. It is to your mind what physical exercise is to your body.

I am going to teach you a meditation exercise. This will help you to relax and focus and also help you feel more of the presence of your guardian angel.

I encourage you to do this as often as you can. This is an exercise that will certainly help you, with practice, to improve.

For this exercise you can take yourself to your

favourite beach and enjoy the beautiful sea views and tranquil setting. You can be in your garden in the sunshine watching the sun glistening in the sky or you can wrap yourself up warm and comfy indoors, imagining you are in your favourite place.

***Make notes about your favourite places you would like to visit to practice meditation.***

_____

_____

_____

_____

**Meditation exercise to learn how to feel the presence of your guardian angel**

Make yourself comfy – you may be sitting or lying down. Perhaps tuck yourself up in a cosy, warm blanket.

> *Close your eyes.*
> *Take ten deep breaths in and out, breathing in through your nose and out through your mouth, relaxing on each out breath.*
> *Say to your guardian angel: 'Thank you guardian angel for your presence, showering me with your gifts in my life every single day.'*

It is important that you give yourself permission during this meditation to feel your guardian angel's presence. It may be in the form of feeling angel tickles or goosebumps, perhaps on your nose or face. Allow the sensations to come in; allow the angel to hug you, to feel their presence.

> *Continue to breathe in through your nose and out through your mouth, relaxing more and more on each breath. Say to yourself, "Relax". Imagine a beautiful white light, the light of your guardian angel, surrounding you right now. Imagine it expanding upwards, raising in you the feeling of happiness that you can communicate with your guardian angel and that you can feel their loving presence.*
> *Breathing in through your nose and out through your mouth, say to yourself, "Relax".*

Your guardian angel – your spiritual best friend – is going to give you an angel hug. Feel their warm, soothing and loving presence. They may even whisper their name to you. You will feel a sense of their love for you.
Hear them say "I am here for you. Ask me for help; I love to help you whenever you need me."

> *Breathing in through your nose and out through your mouth, say to yourself, "Relax".*

You will begin to feel a lovely aura surrounding you.
You will feel the physical presence of your angel, those
tickles on the top of your head, on your face or all over.

> *Breathing in through your nose and out through*
> *your mouth, say to yourself, "Relax".*
> *Ask your guardian angel if they have a message*
> *for you today.*

The message may be simply their loving presence,
shown by an angel tickle or it may come in the form of
an idea or words floating in your head.

> *Take a big breath in and out and slowly open*
> *your eyes. Wiggle your toes and your fingers and*
> *slowly come around, noticing your surroundings.*

If you have been lying on your back, you may like to
roll onto your side with your knees bent. Take your
time and stay longer in that position if you need to.

**TIP!**

**I always recommend having a glass of water or a cup**
**of herbal tea following a meditation.**

## Ask yourself these questions:

How did you feel after this meditation?

_____

_____

Did you feel your guardian angel's presence?

_____

_____

Did your guardian angel whisper their name to you?

_____

_____

Did you receive a personal message from your angel?

_____

_____

_____

Spend some time thinking about the answers to these questions and make notes here.

_____

_____

_____

_____

_____

_____

_____

Try this meditation again another day. The more you practice, the closer you will feel to the presence of your guardian angel.

**Affirmations**

**What is an affirmation?**
They are statements that are repeated to encourage and uplift you as you are speaking them. Positive affirmations, which we are going to use here, are so much more than just feel good quotes and positive statements. They are in the present tense: "I will", "I

am", etc. Your brain will respond to these present tense statements. We speak them as fact and as truth. We use emotional words to evoke feeling. Repeated daily, positive affirmations are a powerful tool for inspiration as well as to remind and reinforce. They help us focus on our goals.

The positive affirmations I have for you to learn (listed on the page 22) are to be repeated daily for at least seven days or longer until you see your clairsentience with your guardian angel increase. If you practice regularly you will see it increase, if not soar!

Here's a tick list to help remind you to complete this for seven days. Colour in the **angel wings** and jot down notes each day about how practising these affirmations made you feel.

| Days 1 – 7 | Notes |
| --- | --- |
| Day 1 | |
| Day 2 | |
| Day 3 | |
| Day 4 | |
| Day 5 | |
| Day 6 | |
| Day 7 | |

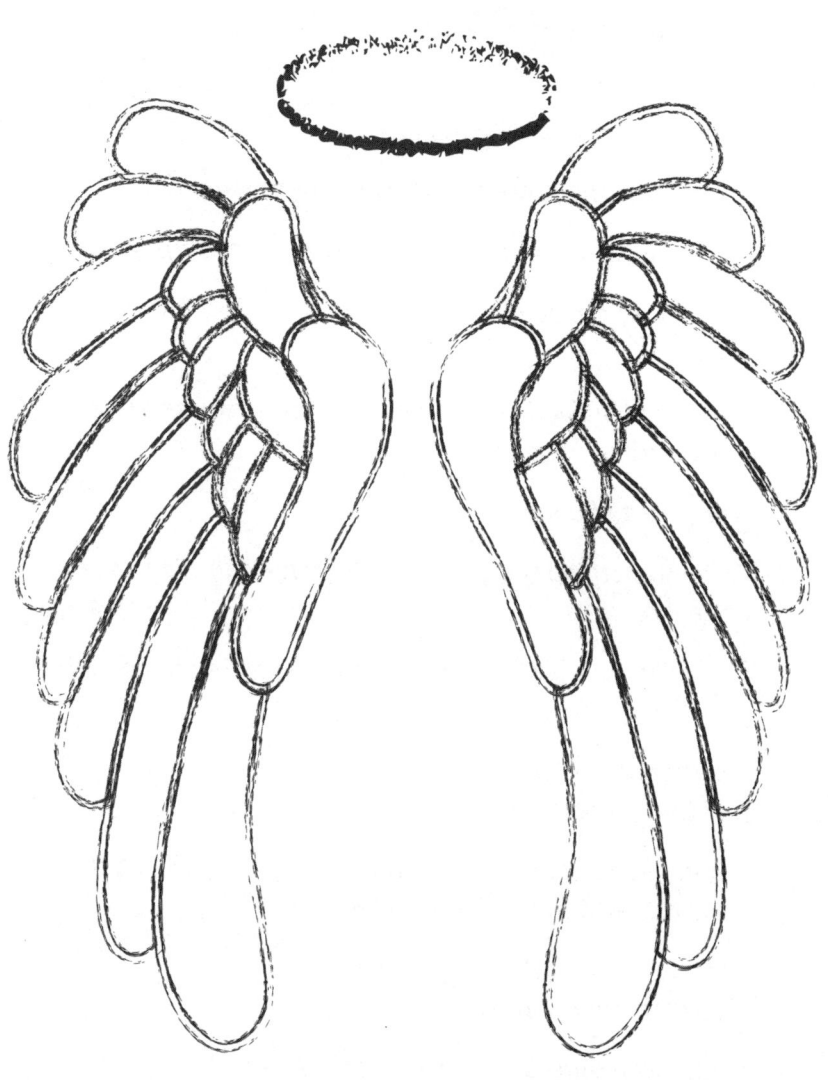

## Positive affirmations to increase your clairsentience

*I give myself permission to feel my guardian angel's presence.*

*I am profoundly clairsentient.*

*I easily feel the presence of my guardian angel.*

*I am a sensitive soul; my sensitivity is my superpower.*

*I am out of the spiritual closet; I don't hide my spiritual side.*

*I am a soul living in a human body, easily connected to my guardian angel.*

*I am free to be me.*

*When something is a good idea, I feel my guardian angel tickle me.*

*When I need to listen and take notice of something, my guardian angel tickles me.*

*The more angel tickles I receive, the more attention I pay to the message.*

*When I have done the right thing, my guardian angel hugs me with their wings of love.*

*I am on the guardian angel frequency; I can feel my guardian angel's presence.*

*I thank you angels, for passing on this gift of clairsentience to me.*

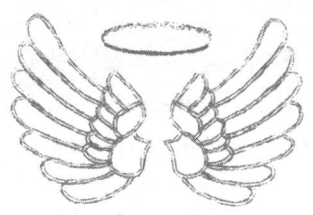

## Chapter 2

*"Believers, look up – take courage.*
*The angels are nearer than you think."*
**Billy Graham**

### Seeing the presence of your guardian angel
### – Clairvoyance

Clairvoyance is the name for seeing your guardian angel's presence, and I know that your angels want you to see these. They will give you visual messages in their own divine way. Here are some signs to look out for:

You may see a vision in your mind which may be a bit like a daydream. It could be in the form of images, movement, floating words in your mind or a picture of happy memories.

Some people experience seeing lights or colours.

Look for signs such as the sun glistening like diamonds on the sea or reflections in a window. Try gazing at a tree in a park or simply looking at some beautiful flowers or plants in your home to help you connect with Mother Earth.

Numbers with significance to you may crop up at unexpected times and in unexpected places.

You could spot a heart shaped cloud or pebble.

If you notice a feather, know that the feather is especially for you as a sign of love, comfort and guidance. It may turn up out of the blue, it may be stuck to something which could make you laugh, or it could be quite profound, especially if it's on a photograph or belonging of a loved one in heaven.

Say to yourself *My ability to see the messages of my guardian angel get stronger every day.*

Give yourself permission to allow these visions to come to you.

Look out for these signs and messages – some will be subtle and others more powerful. This is angel guidance to learn how to notice your angel messages and to take action.

Make a note as a reminder of anything you have spotted here.

_____

_____

_____

_____

Give yourself permission to see these signs. Ask your guardian angel to help you see their signs more clearly.

**Say out loud:** *I give myself permission to see the signs from my guardian angel as a visual sign that I am on the right path. I give myself permission to take positive guided action on the visions I see.*

**An exercise to strengthen your clairvoyance**
In Chapter 1 we learned about meditation and positive affirmations. This exercise combines the two.
In the same way as for the meditation, make yourself comfy; perhaps tuck yourself up in a cosy warm blanket. You may be sitting or lying down. You could be indoors or out in the sunshine, in a park or on a beach. Find a place where you are able to fully relax.

*And close your eyes.*

*Take ten deep breaths in and out, breathing in through your nose and out through your mouth, relaxing on each out breath.*

*Give yourself permission to experience your clairvoyance, to allow yourself to see the messages from your guardian angel.*

*Say out loud or silently to yourself, which ever feels good for you:*

*"I give myself permission to see the signs from my
guardian angel as a visual sign that I am on the right
path.*
*I give myself permission to take positive guided action
on the visions I see.*
*I am deeply clairvoyant."*

*Breathe in and out and relax.*
*Don't worry if you feel any resistance; this is
completely normal to begin with. Just repeat the
following:*

*"It is safe for me to see the messages from my guardian
angel.*
*It is safe for me to see the messages from my guardian
angel.*
*It is safe for me to see the messages from my guardian
angel."*

*Breathe in and out and relax.*
*How do you feel now?*
*When you feel completely relaxed, allow yourself
to daydream.*
*Allow your guardian angels to surround you with
a bright light.*

*Repeat the affirmations and gradually feel the
strengthening of your aura. You will start seeing
signs and messages more clearly. Let all visions,
words and pictures float through your mind. This
will help your spirit to soar like an eagle and
begin to strengthen the visual messages your*

*angels are sending to you.*

*You may experience a bright light expanding and surrounding you. Let this light hug you and surround you with your guardian angel's love. Allow yourself to see beautiful places: the countryside, the rolling hills, the beach, the waves in the sea. Notice all the things you love about being able to see these places in your mind.*

*Breathe in and out and relax.*

*Notice any messages that may appear. These messages could be linked to an idea you've been thinking about for ages that you've not done anything about, or a person you need to contact, or memories of a loved one.*

*Know deep in your soul that these are messages for you from your guardian angel. Don't doubt them.*

*Say to yourself:*

*"My ability to see the messages of my guardian angel gets stronger every day.*

*My ability to see the messages are my guardian angel get stronger every day.*

*My ability to see the messages from my guardian angel get stronger every day."*

Receive with open arms this gift of guidance from your guardian angel. Use the space on the next page to write down the thoughts and ideas that came to you during this meditation.

> Think about what these messages mean to you.
> Think about what these messages are asking you to do.
> Think about the positive action you can take.

## Journal with your Angel

_____

_____

Have confidence knowing that these are signs guiding you in your choice of action.

Positive affirmations are so powerful that we are going to continue with more of these to help you build your clairvoyance with your guardian angel.

Again, repeat the exercise on the next page for seven days or more.

Here's a tick list to help remind you to complete this for seven days. Colour in the **angel wings** and jot down notes each day about how practising these affirmations made you feel.

| Days 1 – 7 | Notes |
|---|---|
| Day 1 | |
| Day 2 | |
| Day 3 | |
| Day 4 | |
| Day 5 | |
| Day 6 | |
| Day 7 | |

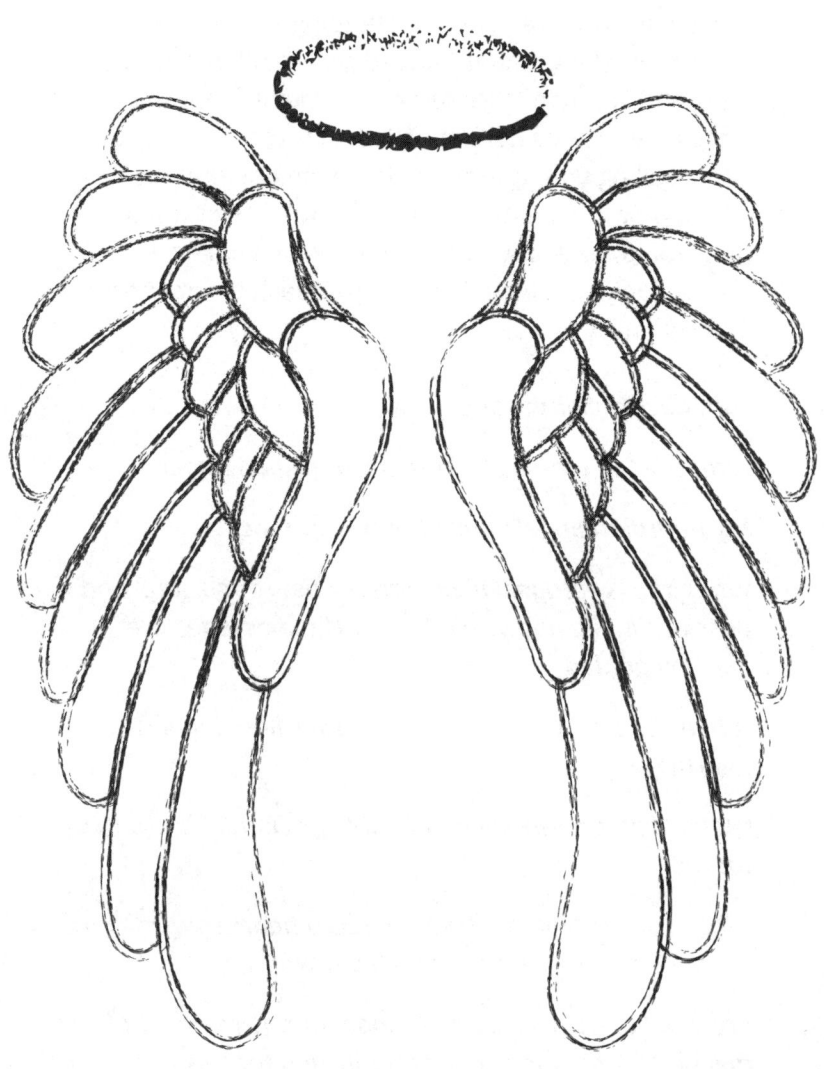

## Positive affirmations to increase your clairvoyance

Make sure you are sitting or standing with good posture, looking straight ahead and that your head, neck and shoulders are relaxed. It might help to imagine you have helium balloons at the top of your head pulling you up. You could be looking out of a window or at a beautiful vase of flowers – or it may help you to look at yourself in a mirror. If using a mirror, look at your reflection after each affirmation and smile.

*I am deeply clairvoyant.*

*I can see the messages from my guardian angel.*

*My guardian angel wants the best for me.*

*When the messages align with my heart and soul, and passions in life and work, I know the messages are divinely guided.*

*When I see a feather, I know my guardian angel is nearby.*

*When I see a heart shaped pebble or cloud, I know it is for me.*

*When I see a sign in a tree such as a heart shaped twig, I know I am loved and supported always.*

*I can call upon my guardian angel at any moment of any day for guidance and support and for this I am truly grateful.*

*I know I am loved and supported always.*

Breathe in and out in between each affirmation, breathing in through your nose and out through your mouth. Relax.

When you are ready, jot down some notes below about what you notice and how this makes you feel. What does this mean to you?

**Journal with your guardian angel**

_____

_____

_____

_____

_____

_____

_____

_____

_____

_____

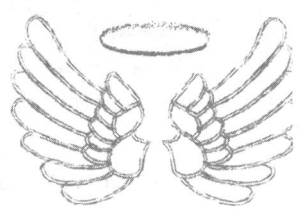

## Chapter 3

*"When you wake up with a song stuck in your head,
it means an angel sang you to sleep."*
**Denise Baer**

### Hearing the messages of your guardian angel – Clairaudience

You may recall a moment when you heard a song on a radio which prompts a memory. Or the words of a song are relevant to something you are experiencing.

Or you are thinking about having a conversation with someone and they call you on the phone at the very same time.

It can be a 'WOW' moment when this happens.

The angels want you to hear these messages and you need to give yourself permission to listen out for them and take notice of any messages given. It's not a coincidence. You may have needed to hear those words at that moment – perhaps you're feeling low, upset about something, not yourself, moody or exhausted. You need to trust that this will pass, and if this is the case, think about what you need to do for you right now. Your guardian angel is always by your side to help. They love to communicate with you. They may point out the lyrics of words in a song that's meaningful to you. The messages given through those words in a song can also be confirmation that you're on the right path and doing the right thing. You can experience this deep within your soul.

Allow yourself to hear the whispers of your guardian angel.

Your guardian angel will not communicate with you in the way another human being will. It is not how they usually operate. To hear them you need to take the time to listen. Our lives can often seem too busy, and we challenge ourselves to do many things at the same time, to get more done when sometimes we really need to ease off and give ourselves room to enjoy each moment. If we can learn to do this and become more aware of our surroundings, we can live in the moment. It will, in return, make our experiences richer.

When you have time to listen more, you will begin to hear more. You will hear more of the signs from your guardian angel.

**An exercise to help you listen more deeply**
Each day take time to stop and listen to the sounds around you. It doesn't matter where you are. Make a conscious effort to note what you can hear. It may be birds, children playing, cars or machines.
What can you hear now? Stop and listen. Jot down notes here if it helps.

_____

_____

_____

When you detect the louder more obvious noises, listen out carefully for the more subtle sounds, such as birds, the rustle of trees, waves on the beach, footsteps, fingers tapping on a keyboard, the quiet humming of a fridge or a person breathing. Learn to heighten your hearing. Tune in to all sounds surrounding you. Listen out for any signs that your guardian angel is near you or communicating with you.

**A quick exercise to hear more sounds of joy**
Listen to the sounds that bring you the most joy in your life. It may be the sounds of the sea, birdsong, or your favourite music – or perhaps you want to hear some quiet or even silence. Choose something that will be calming for your mind and body. Meditation music works well.
You can either sit or lie down.

> *Breathe in and out, in through your nose and out through your mouth, relaxing more and more on each out breath.*

This exercise is perfect for taking a short break in between meetings, in the car before starting or heading home from work, or just to take time out to relax. You'll be amazed how quickly you will learn to do this exercise anytime and anywhere. I am sure you will soon realise how a quick exercise can improve the way you feel. Use it to relax or to calm yourself down during the day. Or use it just for the sheer enjoyment of listening to your favourite sounds. It will help you to focus your hearing too!

Make notes here of your favourite sounds or sounds you want to listen to more often.

_____

_____

_____

_____

**Journal with your Angel**

What sounds bring you joy?

_____

Is it birdsong?

_____

Sounds of the rain?

_____

Sounds of a river?

_____

The roar of a waterfall?

_____

Sounds of the calm of a forest or woods?

_____

Cats purring?

_____

The sound of your favourite animal?

Children playing?

The sound of laughter?

Sounds of the city?

The sound of singing?

Sounds of your family and friends?

The sound of your loved one sleeping?

The sound of your breathing during meditation?

The sound of your favourite music?

Why not create your very own Angel Play List?

Close your eyes and hear these sounds. Capture every laugh and every smile as a sacred memory. Collect them, remember them and savour every single favourite sound with gratitude. The angels will guide you and love you to feel the happiness and healing through doing this exercise. They know it's good for you to slow down, take note and listen to the sounds that give you joy.

When you are completely relaxed after doing the previous exercise, I would like you to do the exercise below. This is where you are going to talk to your guardian angel directly and listen out for any messages or responses.

**An exercise to talk to and listen to the messages of your guardian angel**

Talk to your guardian angel. Start by saying hello and thank them for being in your life. Thank them for guiding you through your journey you are taking.

Wait for a response. Be patient.

They may respond in whispers. Don't be afraid to ask your angels to speak louder or to turn up their volume so you can hear their messages better.

They are listening to you too!

Sitting or standing up, at home, or wherever feels right for you, whether it's out for a walk in nature or the garden, at home in the living room, or in the bathroom, it doesn't matter where, you choose.

> *Close your eyes and take ten breaths in and out. Breathe in through your nose, breathe out through your mouth, and relax.*

I now ask you to read and say aloud the following angel prayer.

### I Talk to Angels Prayer

*Guardian angel, please surround me with your unconditional love; shine your bright light on me for guidance, for positivity, healing, happiness and inspiration. Let your light shine on me like the sun, in my life and my work. Guardian angel, please help me to talk to you and to receive your guidance and love.*

Pause and Smile.

*Guardian angel, please help me hear what you'd like me to hear right now.*
*With gratitude, I thank you.*

Listen out for the guidance you receive.
You can also ask a question or say to your guardian angel *"What would you like me to hear today?"*
You could ask them a question where there are

only two possible answers of either 'yes' or 'no'. Close your eyes, relax and allow yourself a few moments to receive the messages.

Write down any messages or guidance you receive. Some of these messages might come to you later.

## Journal with your angel

Write down any messages you receive from your guardian angel about the answers to the following questions. Make a note of the guidance you hear about these questions. It may seem like a word or words floating towards you – a bit like little whispers. This guidance you receive from your guardian angel will always be helpful, positive and often healing for you.

Ask your guardian angel to help you tune into what to listen out for more in your life

What are you guided to listen to right now?

_____

Are you guided to listen to music?

_____

Are you guided to listen to the radio or a particular programme?

_____

Are you guided to listen to something on TV?

_____

Are you guided to listen to an audiobook?

_____

Are you guided to listen to a meditation?

_____

Are you guided to listen to a podcast?

_____

Are you guided to listen to an interview, a
conversation or a lecture of wise teachings?

_____

Make a plan of action to put into practice any ideas
that came from this exercise. Your guardian angel will
guide you.

_____

_____

_____

_____

_____

_____

_____

_____

To help increase your clairaudience with your guardian angel, repeat the following positive affirmations for seven days, or longer if needed.

*I give myself permission to hear the messages from my guardian angel.*

*I listen well.*

*I'm on the angel wavelength. I can hear my guardian angel talk to me.*

*I can hear my guardian angel's messages.*

*Clairaudience is easy for me.*

Here's a tick list to help remind you to complete this for seven days. Colour in the **angel wings** and jot down notes each day about how practising these affirmations made you feel.

| Days 1 – 7 | Notes |
| --- | --- |
| Day 1 | |
| Day 2 | |
| Day 3 | |
| Day 4 | |
| Day 5 | |
| Day 6 | |
| Day 7 | |

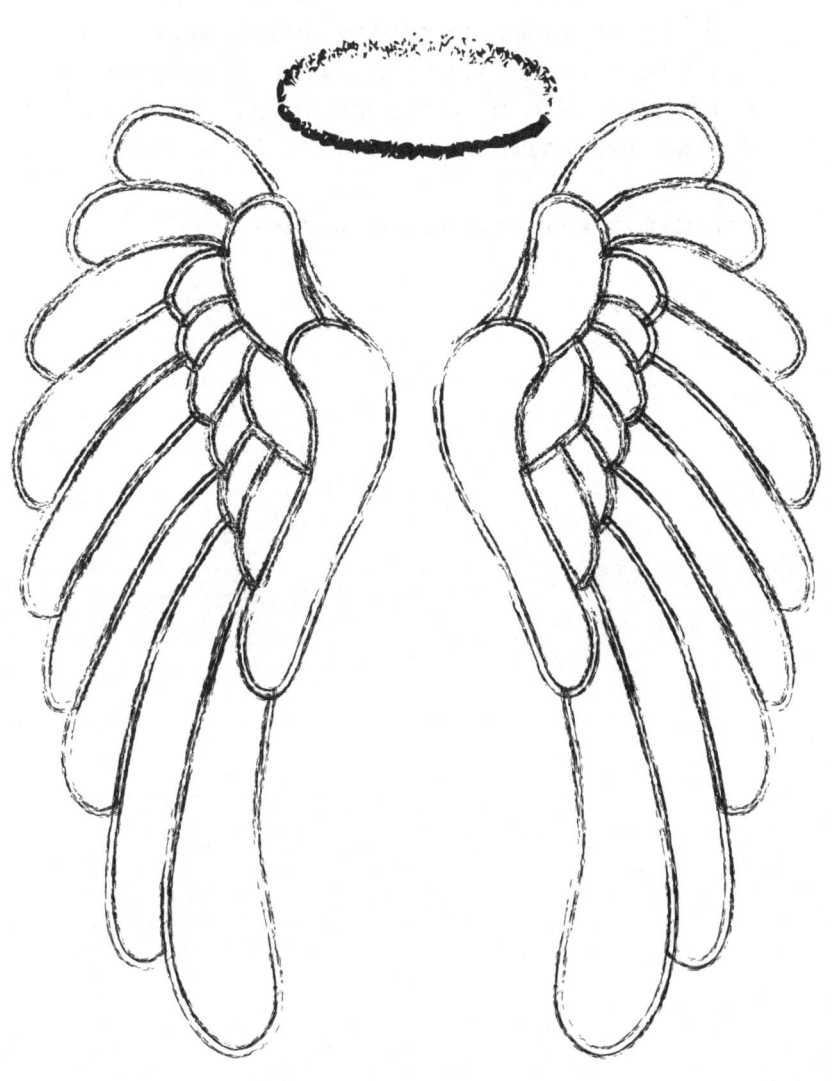

Listening more closely to your family and friends, being aware of your surroundings, your heart and soul, and practicing more positive affirmations and meditations will help you learn to focus. Trust in the divine guidance from your guardian angel and trust in your dreams to help you plan and reach your goals.

**Journal with your angel and keep notes**

_____

_____

_____

_____

_____

_____

_____

_____

_____

_____

_____

_____

_____

_____

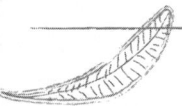

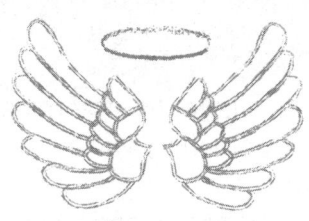

# Chapter 4

*"Whether you've seen angels floating around your bedroom or just found a ray of hope at a lonely moment, choosing to believe that something unseen is caring for you can be a life-shifting exercise."*
**Martha Beck**

**Knowing the messages of your guardian angel – Claircognizance**

Claircognizance is the word for knowing your angel's messages or simply clear thinking. Let's delve a little deeper into what this means.

One of the least understood ways of communicating with your guardian angel is through simply knowing you have a message, without any clarity as to what the message is. It is like a magnetic pull that draws you to something and you just don't know why. Be reassured: these messages are always positive for you and yet they might not make sense at the time.

Have you ever experienced this?

♡ Knowing that a great idea will work without being able to explain why.

♡ Knowing the answer to something without knowing why or where you gained that information.

♡ Meeting a new person and knowing details about them without having met them before.

When these things happen, we can't explain how we know or where we gained the information from, but we trust in ourselves that we know. We sometimes call these moments 'hunches' or 'light bulb moments'. These are messages that we have received through angel communication which we receive, sometimes unknowingly, when our minds are receptive. The more you learn to trust in these messages of guidance the richer your life will be.

If you are looking to receive this help from your guardian angel in the form of a clear plan of action mapped out from beginning to end, this is not how the angels tend to work. However, they will be there to help you throughout your life's journey.

When everything around you is constantly changing its sometimes challenging to know what to do. You cannot change the actions of other people and there will be circumstances in your life that are just out of your control. What you can focus on is *you*. You can focus on you and the steps you need to take along the way. Your guardian angel and surrounding angels will be there to guide you.

Your angels want you to enjoy each moment of each day as much as possible. Think of it as help you need *in the moment* rather than something that might happen next week or month. Concentrating on the here and now and on messages you are receiving will help you to have more clarity over the decisions you are making each day.

Trust in the guidance you receive and keep notes of any messages you receive.

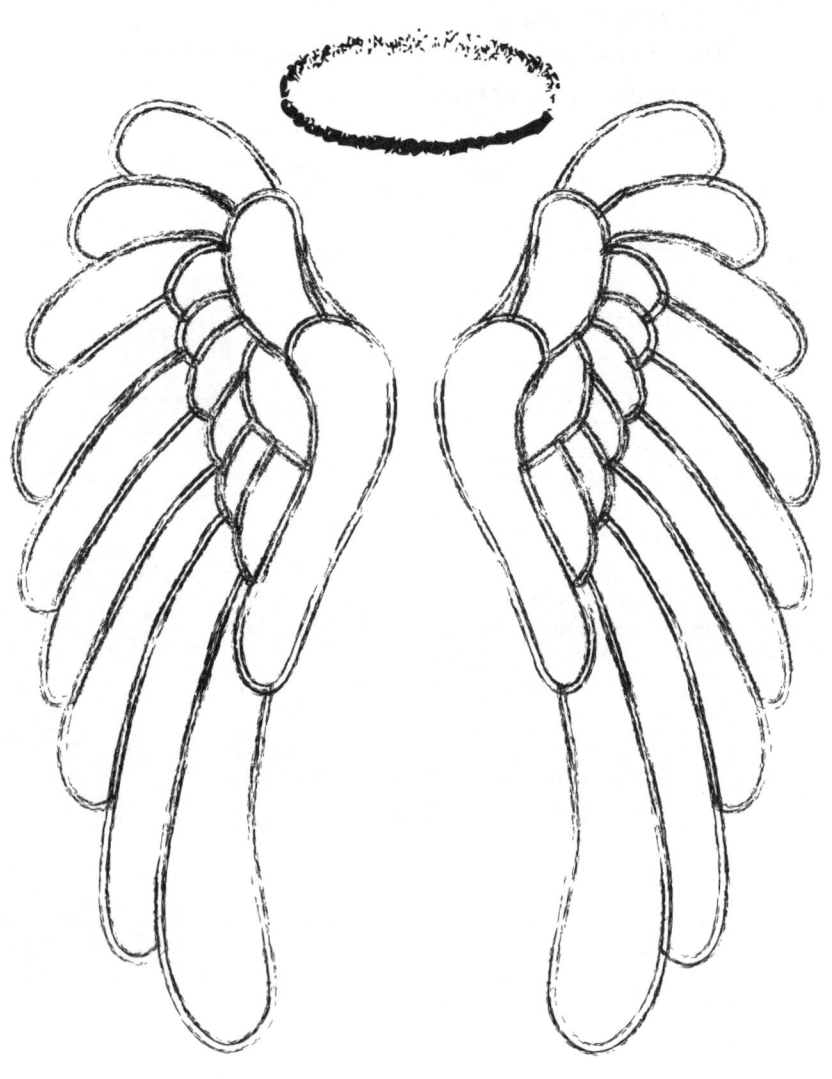

## Here are some tips to help with clear thinking

Although these are so obvious, most of us need to do more of the following to help us relax. Take some time out for you. This is so important, especially if you are a natural worrier or a workaholic! You feel you have too many thoughts buzzing around in your head and sometimes even too many ideas and not enough time to fit it all in. I ask you to ask your angel to help you pick three activities from the list below that you can do this week and colour in the angel wings to show your success. Makes notes about how you feel during and after this time.

- Take time out
- Go for a phone-free walk
- Plan regular time off from work
- Exercise
- Meditate
- Try something new, like water sports
- Learn to play a musical instrument
- Take a bath, light a candle, relax
- Visit the coast and paddle in the sea
- Take a run in the park
- Play games
- Enjoy the company of family and friends

**Journal with your angel**

The three activities I chose were...

1.

_____

_____

2.

_____

_____

3.

_____

_____

Make sure you take time to repeat these activities and ask your guardian angel for guidance. Take guided action from the angels to create a healthy work life balance with time for you to relax and enjoy, especially your time out with the angels.

**An exercise to help with knowing and clear thinking**

One of the ways you can sharpen your knowing and clear thinking is to ask yourself questions and wait to receive the answers from your guardian angel.
Try this daily.
Start by choosing a question that is easy like "Shall I have a bath or a shower?" You may get a message giving you a one-word answer, you may get the word

flash up in your mind. Your angel may give you a sign, like tickling your nose or face, to help with your answer.

**Journal with your angel here**

**Day 1:** I asked this question:

My angel's message was:

**Day 2:** I asked this question:

My angel's message was:

**Day 3:** I asked this question:

My angel's message was:

**Day 4:** I asked this question:

My angel's message was:

**Day 5:** I asked this question:

My angel's message was:

_____

**Day 6:** I asked this question:

_____

My angel's message was:

_____

**Day 7:** I asked this question:

_____

My angel's message was:

_____

## A visualisation to help with clear thinking

Wherever you are, be it at the office, work, at home, in bed, or out and about in nature, sit, stand or lie down for this visualisation and remember to invite your guardian angel to join you.

> *Close your eyes and then take ten breaths in and out, in through your nose and out through your mouth, relaxing on each out breath.*
> *Relax.*
> *Imagine yourself in a favourite place; enjoy being there and knowing how happy you are to be there. Allow yourself to daydream about it for a moment.*

> *Know how you feel being there, allowing your thoughts to be calm and peaceful about this experience and place.*
>
> *Give yourself permission to lap up the happiness and calm and peace you receive from going there in your mind right now.*
>
> *Breathe in the happiness and breathe out. Breathe in the peace and calm and breathe out. Know in your heart that you can enjoy this moment for you right here and right now.*

At this point when you are completely relaxed, ask your guardian angel for a knowing, clear thinking message.

You may simply know what your angel wants you to know or you may receive the message through thoughts that just pop into your head.

It's a brilliant and angelic way to receive messages. It may be an opportunity to daydream about other things you'd like to bring into your life, such as a retreat or holiday you'd love to go on or even are already going on. You can ask for messages and guidance about this, too.

To finish this exercise, say to yourself, *"I allow myself time for thinking as well as resting and relaxing in my life."*

> *Enjoy taking another ten breaths in and out as you daydream about the messages, enjoying this moment, breathing in through your nose and out through your mouth as you relax.*

**TIP!**
**As a deep thinker your mind needs to take a rest. Give it a break and simply be, breathe, and relax. In silence take 30 breaths in and out to calm your mind and body. Try this morning and night.**

Take time to write down any thoughts or messages you received during these exercises.

_____
_____
_____
_____
_____
_____
_____
_____
_____
_____

And to finish this chapter, here are your affirmations to be repeated for at least seven days, or longer if needed.

## Affirmations to increase your clear thinking

*I take time to rest.*

*I take time to relax.*

*I spend more time being (not always trying to do something or to get somewhere).*

*I give myself permission to breathe more slowly.*

*I give myself permission to relax.*

*I give myself permission to switch off my phone more.*

*I give myself permission to turn off social media for at least an hour a day.*

*I give myself permission to switch off my laptop or computer and take time out.*

*I give myself permission to take time off and holidays.*

*I am proud of myself to take time out to be a thinker.*

*I make time for my angels.*

*I make more time just for ME.*

Here's a tick list to help remind you to complete this for seven days. Colour in the **angel wings** and jot down notes each day about how practising these affirmations made you feel.

| Days 1 – 7 | Notes |
| --- | --- |
| Day 1 | |
| Day 2 | |
| Day 3 | |
| Day 4 | |
| Day 5 | |
| Day 6 | |
| Day 7 | |

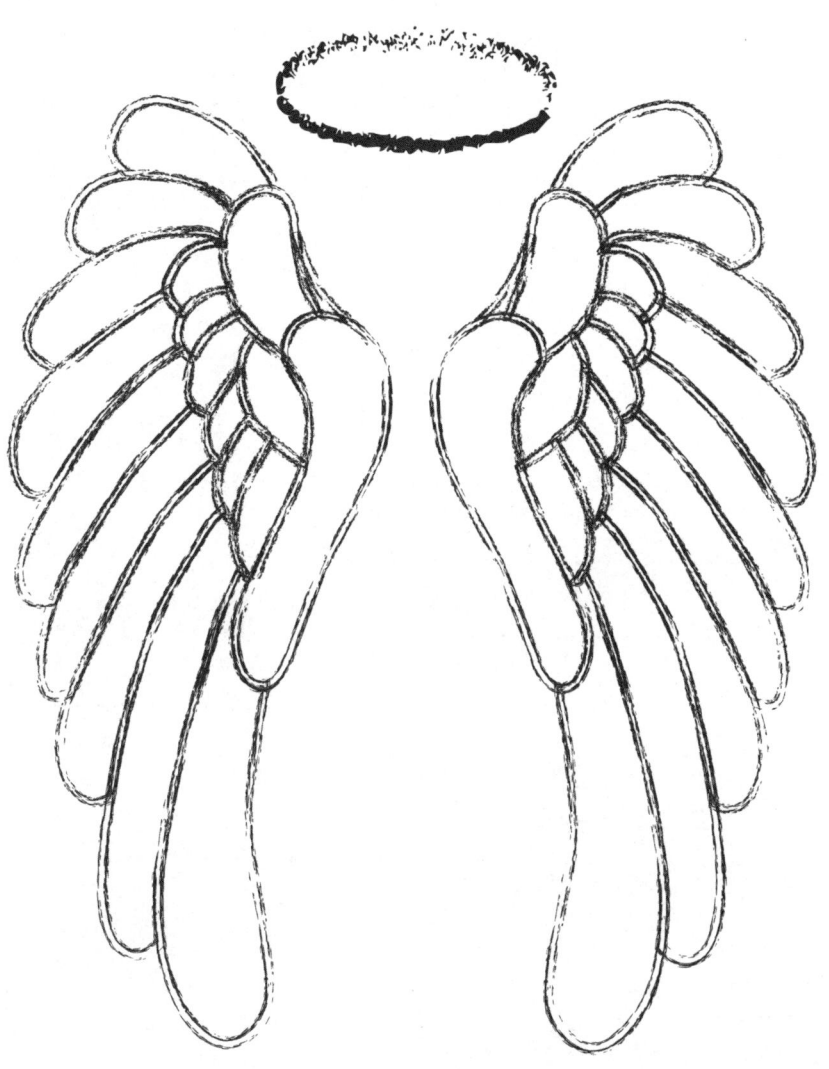

# PART TWO

In Part One we focused on the four main ways your angels communicate with you and hopefully by now you will have started to see, to hear, to feel and to know more of the presence of your guardian angel.

You may be lucky enough to have experienced receiving more than one sign or message at the same time. I am hoping that you are also regularly talking to your angels. They love to hear from you.

**TIP!** **Always remember, you can ask your guardian angel questions at any time. It's a two-way conversation! Be patient though, sometimes it takes time for them to provide you with answers.**

You have been encouraged to keep notes and regularly journal with your guardian angel. By now you will have built up lots of thoughts and ideas and have begun to realise that journaling with your guardian angel is like having a superpower that helps you through the good, challenging and sad times of life, to make it better.

In Part Two we are going to reflect on what we have learnt so far. I am going to introduce new ideas such as how to create your very own angel altar, and how to use candles and angel cards to enhance your connection, as well as how to develop a daily angel routine.

We are also going to look in more detail at how we can use our connection with our angels to help with our everyday lives. For example, how to deal with loneliness, forgiveness, and relationships, as well how we can use what we have learnt to help the children in our lives.

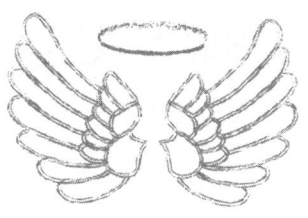

**Chapter 5**

*"I'm trying to shut up and let my angels speak to me
and tell me what I'm supposed to do."*
**Patrick Swayze**

**Communicating with your angels**

Let's begin by looking more closely at what you have
experienced so far by asking yourself these questions
and writing down your answers.

When you felt the presence of your guardian angel,
what were you thinking?

_____

_____

_____

_____

_____

What were you doing?

_____

_____

Who were you talking to?

_____

_____

What were you or they saying when you felt your
guardian angel's clairsentience?

_____

_____

Have you felt the presence of angel tickles? If so, were
they on your head, face, nose, legs, ear, all over, or a
feeling of warmth?

_____

_____

_____

_____

What ideas popped into your head at this time?

_____

_____

_____

What positive action steps are you going to take?

_____

_____

_____

Whatever it was you felt, be reassured it was your guardian angel giving you a nudge. Giving you a sign that it's a good idea or clarity not to do something you've been thinking about. Use any snippets of information in a practical way and don't dismiss them. Take notice and take guided action. It may make all the difference.

This is a lovely little reminder of your connection with your guardian angel as well as a practical reminder of how you are going to use this in your plan of action. The angels want you to achieve your goals and ambitions and to be happy and fulfilled in your life.

If you are still struggling to connect with your guardian angel, practice the following affirmations.

Write these down or print this out and stick it on the wall or fridge or somewhere you will see them and say them every day.

**Positive Affirmations**

*I talk to my guardian angel every day.*

*I give myself permission to experience what my guardian angel is saying to me.*

*I communicate with ease with my guardian angel.*

*Life gets better the more I notice the signs.*

*The angel prayer enriches my life.*

*I say the angel prayer daily.*

*The more I practice, the more easily I communicate with my guardian angel.*

*I love to meditate with my guardian angel; this strengthens my intuition and abilities.*

*I am grateful for my guardian angel; they are my spiritual best friend.*

*I write down any messages I receive from my guardian angel in this book to reassure me that I am connecting with my angels. I do this daily during the good, challenging and sad times of life and it will make my life better.*

My angel journey notes...

_____

_____

_____

_____

_____

_____

_____

_____

_____

_____

_____

_____

_____

_____

_____

_____

_____

## Angel cards

Angel cards are a wonderful way to receive insight and guidance from your angel into your life. They provide gentle messages to support us in our relationships and careers, to help us in decision making, and sometimes just to guide us and give us hope and peace of mind.

There are plenty of Angel Card decks available, each with different imagery. Some have images and some just have a few words. You can pick the deck you are most drawn to, or you can find my Angel Cards Angelic Meaning cards at www.angeliclifestyle.com

To use them, hold them in your hands and touch them to pass on your energy. Ask the angels to bless them and guide you.

### How to pick your angel card?

Simply start by talking to your guardian angel with your angel prayer:

*Guardian angel, please surround me with your unconditional love; shine your bright light on me for guidance, for positivity, healing, happiness and inspiration. Let your light shine on me like the sun, in my life and my work. Guardian angel, please help me to talk to you and to receive your guidance, love and blessing with my angel cards.*
*With gratitude, I thank you.*

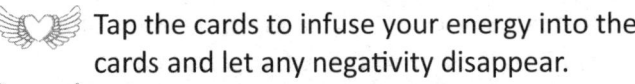 Tap the cards to infuse your energy into the cards and let any negativity disappear.

Shuffle the cards, ask your guardian angel to guide and tell you when to stop shuffling (you may just know when to stop – you may have a feeling it's time to stop shuffling, or you may feel like the word stop has just floated into your mind in a clear thinking way. Trust this.

Slide and whizz the cards along a table or floor.

Ask your angel, "Which is the best card message for me today?"

Notice which card you're guided to; it will always be the correct card message for you.

If you have time, journal about what it means to you and ask your guardian angel for guidance too, and what extra personal message they have for you. Trust what you get and write it down.

## A lovely way to share this with others

Arrange to telephone or FaceTime a friend or family member and pick a card and talk about what it means to you both. Ask your friend or family member, "*What does the card message mean to you?*" Give them a chance to reply and really listen to what they're saying; it really creates positive conversations and a chance for someone to truly express how they feel – and sometimes a chance to bring up things in conversation that they need or want to in an environment that's truly surrounded by the angelic presence of your guardian angel, which somehow makes it much better! Then it's your turn to pick a card for you, and talk with your friend or family member about what it means to you. Have a conversation about it. It can help with your relationships and conversations, creating positivity and happiness all round.

**Create your angel altar**
I am going to show you how to create a special place for you to spend time with your guardian angel.
The angel altar can be on a chest of drawers in the bedroom or wherever feels 'right' for you. Your angel altar is important. This is a place where you can pray, meditate and feel more connected to your guardian angel. Angels are messengers of God and they are a heavenly helper. Having an altar will help you focus on the love, guidance, help and support and joy that's freely available to you. Choose your own special things to go on your altar and make it a place where you love to spend time.

**Ideas for your angel altar:**

 Angel cards

 Positive affirmation cards

 Any deck of oracle cards that you love

 Candles (don't leave them unsupervised) or electric candles

 Twinkly lights

 Picture of an angel, angel statue, or crystal angel

Vision board with your goals and dreams

 Angel manifestation box (see Chapter 12 on manifestation)

 Feathers

 Meaningful signs you have kept, such as a heart-shaped pebble

 Incense and incense holder

 Photos of your favourite spiritual teachers

 Essential oils and an electric oil burner or favourite oil burner

 A peace lily

 Fresh flowers

 A wand!

Decorate it in ways that bring YOU joy.

**TIP!**

**You could also take a picture of it and use it as a screen saver on your mobile phone or laptop so you have it to look at and focus on wherever you are.**

### A daily angel morning and evening routine

The angels love you to have a morning and evening routine, one where you take time for you to connect to your spirit, heart and soul and your guardian angel. This can be five minutes or an hour; it doesn't matter so long as you dedicate regular or daily time to it.

This will help you to improve your life and be able to cope better during the stressful, sad or challenging moments. Solutions will appear so much more easily when you dedicate the time to connecting and receiving help from your angels.

Life is like the waves of the sea, it can be up one day and down the next and it's ok to not always be on top form all the time, and in reality, no one is. Your angel loves to help you and creating daily routines will help. Here are some ideas for creating your morning and evening routine.

**Ideas for your morning routine**
Every morning, first thing, say your angel prayer:

*Guardian angel, please surround me with your unconditional love; shine your bright light on me for guidance, for positivity, healing, happiness and inspiration. Let your light shine on me like the sun, in my life and my work. Guardian angel, please help me to talk to you and to receive your guidance and love with starting my day in a positive way.*
*With gratitude, I thank you.*

This is one great way to set you up for the day and deepen your connection straight away to your guardian angel, you may get a tingly nose even after reading just a few lines, meaning you have felt your guardian angel, which is incredible and will hopefully become the norm for you with practice. I still feel a sense of wonder every time! This gives you a chance to talk, connect with your angel at the start of your day. They are ready and waiting. You could also try any of the following;

1. Meditate. Lying down or sitting, close your eyes and take 10-30 breaths in and out; a few minutes of quiet time to breathe and relax. Close your eyes, breathe in through your nose, and as you exhale through your mouth, relax.

2. Pick an angel card and a positive affirmation card first thing as part of your routine and think about what these messages means to you.

3. Visualise. Write down a goal or something you want to achieve, however small or big. Close your eyes for a few minutes and visualise it in detail. Let your mind daydream about how wonderful you will feel when you reach this goal.

4. Journal with your guardian angel. Write down what came up for you in your visualisation or daydream and anything you feel inspired or guided to write about. Put some short bullet point action steps to take.

5. Take time to read something you're inspired to read. Ask your guardian angel which book, page or chapter to read.

6. Take up some regular exercise such as pilates or yoga, or just go out for a walk in the fresh air (perfect for cardiovascular exercise, blowing the cobwebs away, a chance to breathe, connect

to your heart, soul and your guardian angel). A magical way to start the day.

Remember: just do what you have time for or can create time for.

**TIP!** **It may be worth getting up an extra 20 minutes earlier to make sure you create time for your new routine.**

*"We are what we repeatedly do. Excellence, therefore, is not an act but a habit."*

**Aristotle**

### Ideas for your evening routine

1.  Take time for relaxation. Lie down on your back on a good mat or blanket with a cushion behind your head, with your knees bent and feet hip width apart for more back support. Place your hands on your tummy, ribcage or out to the side if that's comfortable for you, palms facing up, either at shoulder height or lower if that feels better. Breathe in through your nose. As you exhale through your mouth, relax, close your eyes and continue the breathing for ten breaths in and out.
2.  If you want to dedicate more time, try using the meditation exercise (page 15).
3.  Enjoy a bath with candles. Gaze at the candles and the flame and think of ten things you are

grateful for that day. Let the flame of the candle amplify your feeling of gratitude.

4. Read your favourite book or perhaps try reading something new like poetry.

5. Have a quiet night in and journal with your guardian angel. Choose a chapter in this book and read over your notes thinking about your angel journey.

6. Spend time at your angel altar or in meditation.

7. Pick an angel card with the guidance of your angel and think about what this means to you or a family member or friend. Pick up the phone, as I am sure they would love to hear from you.

These are just a few ideas for your evening routine. Take some time for you every evening to relax and enjoy, even if it's only for a short while. You deserve it.

## Using candles

### Guardian Angel candle exercise

 Light a candle.

 Gaze at the candle.

 Take ten breaths in and out, breathing in through your nose and out through your mouth.

 Relax on each out breath whilst gazing at the light, bright, beautiful candle.

Say your angel prayer:

*Guardian angel, please surround me with your unconditional love; shine your bright light on me for guidance, for positivity, healing, happiness and inspiration. Let your light shine on me like the sun, in my life and my work. Guardian angel, please help me to talk to you and to receive your guidance and love through the light of this candle.*
*With gratitude, I thank you.*

Thank your guardian angel for being in your life, thank yourself for all the good you've done in your life and happiness that's already in your life, both in the past and right now.

Ask your guardian angel for a message and allow it to come in through seeing, hearing, feeling and knowing the messages.

Continue breathing in through your nose and out through your mouth, gazing at the candle flickering with its bright, pretty light.

What messages came to you?

It might be a word or words such as slow down, rest, relax, or it might be a message to take more care of yourself, take a holiday or a retreat. Allow yourself to daydream about this as you gaze at the candle. It can be thoughts about anything, even work inspiration!

If you enjoyed this candle exercise, do this regularly, and act as you have been guided to by your angels.

When you have a spare five minutes or more, sit with your angel journal and write what came to you and anything else your guardian angel wanted you to know. TRUST what came to you, and write it down: this is key.

**Journal with your guardian angel**

_____

_____

_____

_____

_____

_____

_____

_____

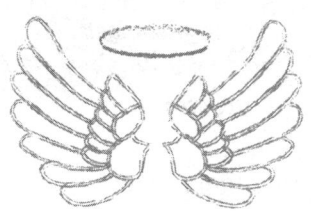

# Chapter 6

*"If you're not okay, you might as well not pretend you are, especially since life has a way of holding us down until we utter that magic word: help!*
*That's when angels rush to your side."*
**Glennon Doyle Melton**

## Asking for help

Asking for help is a sign of strength. Being a human isn't always easy and that's an understatement. The angels love to help you, especially your guardian angel. Though you can always be your own best friend, it's always nice to know your angels can be by your side, at the drop of a hat, when times get tough. Life does get better most days when you work and connect with the angels, but remember we are on this journey together. No one is 'perfect', despite what we may see portrayed on social media. We all have feelings, struggles in life, and family that we might not always get on with, and that's normal too. The point is that you can ask for help, for heavenly guidance at any time and it will be there for you, I promise, and often in a flash.

## Ask yourself these questions

Start off with your angel prayer:

*Guardian angel, please surround me with your unconditional love; shine your bright light on me for guidance, for positivity, healing, happiness and inspiration. Let your light shine on me like the sun, in my life and my work. Guardian angel, please help me to talk to you and to receive your guidance and love. With gratitude, I thank you.*

> Place your hands on your heart. Close your eyes and take ten relaxing or energising breaths in and out before you start. Breathe in through your nose and breathe out through your mouth, relax on each out breath.

Ask your angel what page or chapter of this book you should read right now. This will give you daily guidance for you to focus on. Trust that those words, those pages will have something meaningful and relevant to guide you in some way in your life right now. Trust this to be true and keep following each piece of guidance along the way. Ask:

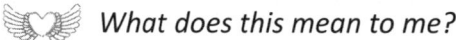 *What does this mean to me?*

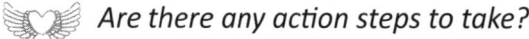 *Are there any action steps to take?*

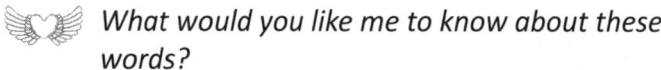 *What would you like me to know about these words?*

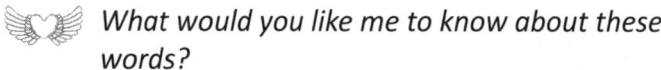 Write what comes to you down in your angel journal pages.

You may be naturally shy, supersensitive, or hate conflict and try to avoid it at all costs. The angels will urge you to use your power to speak up, to reply with assertiveness and kindness – even if it takes you a few days to pluck up the courage! Always do what feels right for you and I am sure you won't go far wrong.

The reality is that angels can help you with all things – all you need to do is take the time to ask, pause, listen and be open to their messages. It could take ten seconds, one minute, five minutes or even longer to hear an answer or some guidance. It's then up to you to do something about it. Take action.

Being guided by your angels, you will see more clearly and feel relief that you're truly never alone. So, whenever you need to, pause, stop what you're doing and take ten breaths in and out, say your angel prayer and ask a question. You will receive an answer and guidance from your angels.

## The ASK Exercise with your Angel

I know you will find the following exercise and question exercise helpful in asking for and receiving help from the angels. Angels often provide help and guidance from other human beings too, because it is important to talk things through with someone you love and trust. You may feel more connected in your convictions and being true to yourself by doing this. Here are the ASK exercise steps to take:

**Step 1** is asking your angel for help.

**Step 2** is being open to receiving a solution. This may involve talking to your guardian angel, taking some time out to meditate or take a walk, or talking to a trusted friend.

**Step 3** is very much about knowing you have a solution. It could be a solution to a challenge, problem, question or situation, even if it's the very first step – and that's OK. Don't worry if you haven't got a completely clear action plan. So long as you're heading in the right direction, a more positive direction, you can breathe easy, feel better instantly and be ready for the next piece of guidance to arrive.

**ASK**

Step 1: **Ask**

Step 2: **Solution**

Step 3: **Know** you'll receive the answer or some beautiful guidance

There are times in life when you just aren't feeling so full of beans; maybe you're feeling a bit flat. It might actually have nothing to do with you – it might be that you've picked up on the mood of those around you in an empathic, sensitive way and you've taken on the feelings of others. This can drain you. Or you've been worrying about a family member and taking on all their problems and concerns. It's all good and well to care, but the angels urge you to look after yourself, because then you'll be able to detach more and help in a more positive, pro-active and inspiring way – as opposed to joining in with other people's lower vibrations. It's good to understand how others are feeling when they're feeling down, but not to end up feeling that way yourself. Here is an exercise that gives you a chance to get things off your chest, to be completely honest with where things are at so that you can reflect on it to then create positive change to feel better. Here we go.

**Angel letter 'to feel better' exercise**

Here's what to do:

1.  Start by saying your angel prayer:

*Guardian angel, please surround me with your unconditional love; shine your bright light on me for guidance, for positivity, healing, happiness and inspiration. Let your light shine on me like the sun, in my life and my work. Guardian angel, please help me to talk to you and to receive your guidance and love. With gratitude, I thank you.*

2.  Write a letter of what you need and want in your life right now. What's wrong? Be honest. Write it to your guardian angel. Write, *Dear guardian angel*, then write your letter and sign it from you at the bottom of the letter.

3.  Once you have finished your letter, replace all the 'I need', 'I want', and any negative words with more positive words or what you're wanting to create in the present tense. You may want to replace the negative words with phrases such as: *I'm grateful for, thank you angels for, I appreciate...*

4.  Be honest, what is the truth really? Is it true what you're saying? For example, if you say you have no good friends, is that *really* true? Or is it that you would like to have more good friends, for example locally? Or perhaps you have some good friends, but you would like to see them or speak to them more often. Remember, it is the quality, not quantity and don't fall into the

trap of comparing yourself to others, it's oh so depressing. If you do, SMILE, acknowledge it and think about what it is that you would like and know deep down that you can create this in your own special, unique way.

5. Rewrite the letter but this time write about what you do want in the present tense, with sentences starting with things like: *Angels I thank you for...* (You fill in the blanks).

6. You may like to shred, drown or burn the original letter. Shredding is quick and easy – you can literally shred it with your hands and tear it up into little pieces. Alternatively, you can get a bowl of water and screw the piece of paper up into a ball, then place it in the water and keep squidging it in the water until the ink starts to run and disappear. If you decide to burn it, do so safely. As you destroy your letter, say to yourself:

*I release this with love.*
*Thank you angels for helping me release my old worries with love.*
*I start afresh.*
*Goodbye to the old, hello to the fresh, sparkly new.*

7. Say each new phrase daily in the mirror for the next twenty-one days, smiling regularly as you do this. Look in your eyes, look at you, and smile at yourself with compassion as you do this. Do it because you want to make a positive difference to your life and everyone and everything around you. Because you will.

**TIP!**

**Louise Hay was the creator of mirror affirmations, so for more in-depth info on this, she's your girl!**

### Asking for help when someone's upset you

When you feel upset by someone else – it may be a friend, family, work colleague, client or even someone on social media – you can ask for help. Remain assertive. Don't hesitate to block someone if they are, for example, leaving unkind, unfriendly or abusive comments on social media. Delete these comments immediately if this happens to you. The angels say, "Remember, they are only words". They have nothing to *actually* do with you. It's all about them (and usually they have upset and anger in their own life which they are offloading on to you). Equally these types of comments can come from a narcissistic or abusive type of person. Do not let it be your focus. Delete them from you radar.

Think of all the people that do like you, that love you and want to be with you, that enjoy your company and appreciate your work. It's sad that some people think it's OK to be unkind or abusive. As a sensitive person you may take it more personally and suddenly make it your only focus. DON'T. Take yourself off for five minutes and go outdoors if you can.

Close your eyes, and say your angel prayer:

*Guardian angel, please surround me with your unconditional love; shine your bright light on me for guidance, for positivity, healing, happiness and inspiration. Let your light shine on me like the sun, in my life and my work. Guardian angel, please help me to talk to you and to receive your guidance and love. With gratitude, I thank you.*

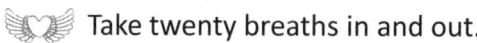 Take twenty breaths in and out.

Imagine the sun is shining; visualise the sun shining. Feel a warm glow of warmth on your skin. Smile. Now imagine you're gazing at the clouds – see the clouds moving and picture your thoughts being able to freely come and go like the clouds. Let your negative thoughts drift off in one cloud, and allow new sparkly, happy thoughts to float in on another. This is your prerogative to choose how you want to feel. Choose happy, choose kind, and choose the best for you. You deserve the best. Your angels want the best for you.

Follow these thoughts with the following meditation.

**I breathe and relax Angel Meditation**

Say to your guardian angel:

*I love feeling calm*

*I breathe and relax (breathing in through your nose and out through your mouth each time)*

*I love smiling*

*I breathe and relax*

*I love laughing*

*I breathe and relax*

*I love feeling grateful*

*I breathe and relax*

*I love the sun*

*I breathe and relax*

*I love gazing at the sky*

*I breathe and relax*

*I love gazing at the clouds as they drift on by*

*I breathe and relax*

*I love seeing the colours of the sun rising*

*I breathe and relax*

*I love how beautiful nature is*

*I breathe and relax*

*I love feeling the presence of my guardian angel*

*I breathe and relax*

*I love seeing my guardian angel*

*I breathe and relax*

*I love hearing my guardian angel whisper positive words of praise to me*

*I breathe and relax*

*I love knowing my guardian angel is always there for me like a best friend*

*I breathe and relax*

*I love life*

*I breathe and relax*

*I love you... (say your name)*

*I breathe and relax*

*I feel better*

*I breathe and relax*

*I feel great!*

*I breathe and relax*

*I feel wonderful*

*I breathe and relax*

*I feel enthusiastic*

*I breathe and relax*

*I am me*

*I breathe and relax*

*I love being me*

*I breathe and relax*

*Hooray!*

*I breathe and relax*

*I love to smile*

*I breathe and relax*

*I love my life*

*I breathe and relax*

*I love feeling energised*

*I breathe and relax*

**TIP!** **You will have to put the work in and do the homework. Remember you and your guardian angel are a team.**

## The healing angel walk

There may be moments and times in your life that certain things feel like they're getting on top of you and this is where you may find it useful to take yourself off on a healing angel walk. You will find that this exercise helps you tremendously in finding answers to your problems. If this works for you, make sure you refer to it again and again throughout your life.

**TIP!** **Remember your guardian angel is always there for you to ask for help, as is this exercise you can use while out on a walk with your guardian angel.**

**What you need:**

⟫ A pen.

⟫ Your angel journal.

⟫ You might want a bag with you.

⟫ And YOU!

**Say your angel prayer:**

*Guardian angel, please surround me with your unconditional love; shine your bright light on me for guidance, for positivity, healing, happiness and inspiration. Let your light shine on me like the sun, in my life and my work. Guardian angel, please help me to talk to you and to receive your guidance and love. With gratitude, I thank you.*

**TIP!**

**If you don't know this off by heart make sure you carry a copy of this in your bag, your pocket or on your phone. It makes a great screen saver!**

Then, as you walk along, think about what you need help with right now.

Stop in a quiet spot on your walk and write your problems down, one at a time. Write how you honestly feel.

 Walk for a little while again, breathing in for a count of four and out for a count of four. Breathe in through your nose and then out through your mouth, relaxing and energising as you exhale, feeling like you are blowing any stress away and breathing in the tranquillity and the solutions all at the same time.

> Say or think:
>
>
> I breathe in tranquillity and solutions.
> I breathe out stress.
> I breathe in peace and calm.
> I breathe out peace and calm.

Your guardian angel will help you come up with solutions, so talk to them and ASK for their help with your problems, challenges or anything disturbing you, such a recurring patterns of behaviour.

 Once you've asked your guardian angel for help, stand (or sit) with your pen and paper and write down what positive solutions come to you. It may be about talking to a relevant practitioner, counsellor or other professional about the situation, or discussing things with a trusted friend or family member.

You might be lucky that your guardian angel immediately helps you find solutions. It may take time, but taking the time to think about the situation and to share this with your guardian angel is so powerful, so positive, and a gentle way of dealing with difficult issues. Trust that the guidance you are writing down is from your guardian angel and your best self, the part of you that always knows what's best; the part of you that shines like a diamond. Because your essence, your soul, really and truly does know what is best for you.

**TIP!**

**Remember that you can sparkle and shine at any moment in your life if you wish to, because it's all 'in there' already. You just need a bit of help from your guardian angel to find it.**

 Walk for a little while again, breathing in for a count of four and out for a count of four. Breathe in through your nose and then out through your mouth, relaxing and energising as you exhale, feeling like you are blowing any stress away and breathing in tranquillity and solutions all at the same time.

Say or think:

⟶ I breathe in tranquillity and solutions.
⟶ I breathe out stress.
⟶ I breathe in peace and calm.
⟶ I breathe out peace and calm.

Thank your angels for their help.

Repeat this process and walk for as long as feels right for you. Remember that different people, situations and aspects of the challenge may crop up, so give yourself some time and space in-between. It's simple.

$\Longrightarrow$ WALK

$\Longrightarrow$ BREATHE

$\Longrightarrow$ RELAX

$\Longrightarrow$ And then journal again and repeat the steps.

After your walk, give yourself permission to write a to-do list of the positive, problem-solving action steps that you have come up with.

**Journal with your angels**

_____

_____

_____

_____

_____

_____

_____

*Asking for help*

## Asking your guardian angel for help with automatic writing

Automatic writing is a way of connecting with your guardian angel. It's like you're writing a letter together. You ask a question and then they reply with an answer. How great is that? So, all you have to do is write down what guidance pops into your mind, or any thoughts and simply let them flow through your pen or pencil. As long as it is positive and helpful, you know the guidance is coming from your guardian angel.

**Say your angel prayer:**

*Guardian angel, please surround me with your unconditional love; shine your bright light on me for guidance, for positivity, healing, happiness and inspiration. Let your light shine on me like the sun, in my life and my work. Guardian angel, please help me to talk to you and to receive your guidance and love with this exercise.*

*With gratitude, I thank you.*

> Take ten breaths in and out and either close your eyes as you do this or light a candle and gaze at the flame flickering as you do this. This is a wonderful focus. Breathe in through your nose and out through your mouth, relaxing more and more on each out breath.

Have a pen ready.

**Ask a question to your guardian angel and write the question down.**
**Write the question here:**

_____

_____

Then, expect to receive a response and immediately put pen to paper and see what comes in response to your question from your guardian angel. Write until you're finished here:

_____

_____

_____

_____

If there are more questions or aspects to the question simply ask that too here:

_____

_____

_____

Once you've finished, thank your guardian angel for their guidance.

> **TIP!**
> **The key is to take some guided action to follow at the relevant time.**
> **Give yourself permission to bring more happiness into every area of your life.**

The angels encourage you to bring happiness and happy moments into every single day of your life. If you ask for more happy moments, focus more on looking and expecting more happiness to arrive and ask yourself *"How can I bring more happiness into both my life and the lives of others today?"*, you will see such a difference.

On a weekly or daily basis, with a day planned, you can ask yourself how you can enjoy more happiness and joy in that area of your life.

Let's look at the seven main areas of your life:

Your health, wealth and money, friends and family, your career, personal and spiritual development, fun and hobbies, and your home.

Pick one area to start with that day, and think to yourself, *"How can I make this part of my life happy and more enjoyable today?"* Try it. It works!

Often, it's about attitude. Even something as simple as planning to be somewhere early, therefore enabling you to have a peaceful journey with plenty of extra time in case of road works or traffic delays, can turn your whole day around.

You can go even further by offering random acts of kindness on the way, such as letting other cars out of junctions and roads and putting a smile on other's faces too. You may find that a small shift in your schedule/planning can make all the difference.

## Asking for help with your friends and family

Ask your angel this question:
*How can I make my relationship with... (insert their name) happy and better today?*
Write down what comes to you – it might surprise you!

_____

_____

_____

_____

_____

_____

**TIP!** Treating others as you wish to be treated yourself and being not just pleasant but being extra smiley and friendly right from the word go with your family and friends (even when you don't feel like it) sets things off on a good footing. It's not about masking your feelings or brushing things under the carpet, it's about creating the life and relationships you want and leading the way.

Ask the angel to help you make your relationships happier in some way. Then take guided action!

## Asking for help with your personal and spiritual development

Ask your angel this question:
*How can I create some happy personal and spiritual development time for me today?*
Write down what comes to you here. It might surprise you!

_____

_____

_____

_____

Ask your angel to help you improve your personal and spiritual development in some way. Then take guided action!

**TIP!** **A brilliant thing that you can implement right now is to create a consistent morning and evening routine that you do on a daily basis. You are committing to this just for you, and yes, you're also committing to enjoying it every single day. The key is to block out some time (whatever amount you can squeeze in) before you start emptying the dishwasher and making the packed lunches! It's your special time that you devote unconditionally to you. A daily retreat. It might mean you set the alarm a little bit earlier or you delegate a household or work task you often do to someone else!**

## Asking for help with your career

Ask your angel this question:
*What one thing can I do in my work today that would make me happier?*
Write down what comes to you here. It may surprise you!

_____

_____

_____

_____

_____

Ask your angel to help you make work happier in some way. Then take guided action!

## Asking for help with having fun today and perhaps making time for a new hobby

Ask your angel this question:
*How can I make my day more fun or do something for me in my spare time? What is this going to be today?*
Write down what comes to you here. It may surprise you!

_____

_____

_____

_____

_____

_____

Ask your angel to help you have more fun or discover a hobby. Then take guided action!

**TIP!**

It isn't necessarily realistic or possible to be going off to clubs, classes and the spa every single day of the week, but there's always something you can do just for you. It might be enjoying a dance in the kitchen, putting some good music on, doing some art and crafts or even learning a language. It might be taking time to play a card game or something else you enjoy, but whatever it is, give yourself permission to do it. If you're able to get out and about it may be going for a run, walk or to an exercise class. You decide. You are the creator of your life, so make sure you do more of what you enjoy!

**Asking for help with your home and how you can make your home happier**

Ask your angel this question:
*How can I make my home life happier today?*

Write down what comes to you here. It may surprise you!

_____

_____

_____

_____

Ask your angel to help you make your home life happier. Then take guided action!

**TIP!** **This can be about all sorts of things; it can be about how tidy, clean, organised and relaxed your home feels, or it may be about having more harmonious relationships within your home. Whatever it is, do more of it to make your home a happier place. It may be always having a bunch of flowers in your home and a bowl of fresh fruit. It might be having a fridge full of tasty food for you and your family. It may be dedicating your spare time to tidy, de-clutter and clean, especially if coming home to a clean house makes you feel happier and more relaxed.**

**Asking for help with your money and wealth**

Ask your angel this question:
_How can I feel better about my wealth and finances today?_
Write down what comes to you, it might surprise you!

_____

_____

_____

_____

_____

Ask your angel to help you feel better about your wealth and finances in some way. Then take guided action!

**Asking for help with your health**

Ask your angel this question:
*What one thing can I do to improve my health and well-being today?*
Write down what comes to you, it might surprise you!

_____

_____

_____

_____

Ask your angel to help you improve your health and well-being in some way. Then take guided action!

**Asking for help with love and romance**

Ask your angel this question:
*What one thing could I do today to bring more love and romance into my life? (*This is especially for you if you're single).
Write down what comes to you, it might surprise you!

_____

_____

_____

_____

Ask your angel to help you with love and romance in some way. Then take guided action!

**TIP!** **This isn't just about love and romance with others, this is about loving yourself too; loving your life and loving yourself the way you are. If you love candles, then light a candle; if you love doing certain things then do more of them! Treat yourself with kindness to create a rich, happy and fulfilling life.**

**Loving hearts angels exercise for a work-life balance**

Get a piece of paper and colouring pens.

→ Write today's date on a piece of paper.

→ Then draw nine hearts on your piece of paper and write the following above each heart:

  ♡ Personal and spiritual development

  ♡ Exercise and hobbies, including pets

  ♡ Money, wealth and abundance

  ♡ Family and friends

  ♡ Self-care

  ♡ Work

  ♡ Home

  ♡ Food and drink

  ♡ Self-love and romance.

→ Write down all the things you currently love that are in your life in each area either in or around the heart.

→ Colour the hearts if you feel inspired.

→ Then in a different colour pen, write down all the things you'd like to bring into your life in each area: your hopes, goals, dreams and aspirations – think big and small.

→ Ask your guardian angel for ideas. Close your eyes, breathe and allow yourself to daydream with your guardian angel about how you'd love your life and work to be in six to twelve months. Daydream about this; relax. Take ten relaxing, calming breaths in and out and imagine and picture all the possibilities. It can be real, in your

mind, or it can be a goal you want to achieve.
Allow these magical thoughts to surround
you like waving a magic wand of happiness,
abundance, health and wealth into your life.
Enjoy the feeling of possibilities. You deserve it.

Keep this paper in your book or journal and read it
regularly to keep you on track to reach your dreams
and achieve your goals. This is a wonderful exercise to
enjoy doing regularly with your angels.

**TIP!**

**The angels love you being happy as often as possible
and they are here to support you in making each day
and moment count, filling all areas of your life with
more happiness and joy. You really can achieve this –
and remember, you are worth it!**

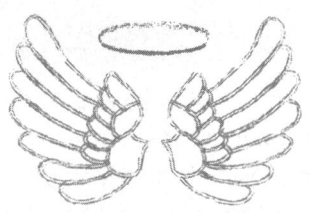

## Chapter 7

*"Make friends with the angels, who though invisible
are always with you.
Often invoke them, constantly praise them,
and make good use of their help and assistance
in all your temporal and spiritual affairs."*
**Saint Francis de Sales**

### You are never alone

There may have been times in your life where you have felt alone. That time may even be right now. You may have experienced being a shy child who didn't have the confidence to say or express how they felt. This may have led you to feeling lonely in certain circumstances, even though you were surrounded by other people. It is difficult sometimes to tell people that we are upset and lonely. Does this sound familiar?

If someone has been unkind, abusive or a bully, you should always tell someone that you trust about it or seek professional advice. These people can be so manipulative and before you know it you could feel isolated and alone. The angels say to always keep in touch with your closest friends and family members and tell the truth to others about what's going on. The angels will support you with this. They want you to live a happy life and they will help you to find the courage to remove these toxic people from your life.

You really are never alone, even during times when it feels like you are. Your guardian angel is always there beside you and has been there with you from birth. Even though you might not be able to see your angel, that doesn't matter at all – that's a skill you could one day develop. You don't have to be able to see them to receive their help. Rest assured they are always there for you and all you need to do is ASK. At times of your life when you're feeling low, stressed, lonely or bereaved you may sometimes forget this. In this book you will find lots of activities and solutions to help you and to remind you to stay in touch with your angels and to notice their unconditional love and guidance.

In this chapter, let's take it a step further with your guardian angel. If you haven't done this before, why not go on a first date with them? I'm not joking! You have already taken a walk with them (in Chapter 6), so why not go out for coffee or lunch with them too? To begin with you can try this at home. You can create special moments to share regularly. Here are a few ideas:

⟶ Breakfast in bed and pick angel cards and journal together.

⟶ Dinner or lunch together – at home you can set them a place if you want to and talk to them or pick angel cards together.

⟶ Watch a film together.

⟶ Go on a picnic together.

⟶ Go on a nature walk together.

⟶ Cycle, run or swim together.

⟶ Boat trip or bus journey.

⟶ Visit a museum.

⟶ Go to the theatre.

The list can be endless.

Feel confident to venture out with your guardian angel by your side. They will always go with you, listen to you and be there to keep you company. Just ask them. They will wait for your invite, as they won't interfere without you asking them. Just like you'd invite a friend or a member of your family to meet up – do the same with your guardian angel. You can share your outings together regularly. Always remember to say thank you for their company and when they have helped you.

You'll soon realise there will never again be a time when you will feel alone!

That's the fun part of knowing your guardian angel is close. However, we also need to look at the more serious issues that affect our lives and sometimes we need that extra bit of help.

There may have been times in your childhood when someone made an unkind remark to you or an abusive or bullying comment that really upset you and you felt alone in the fact that you just didn't know how to talk about this to anyone. Not even being able to talk to your favourite teacher or relative can make you feel incredibly lonely. The angels DO NOT want this for you. They want you to feel confident about feeling and expressing your emotions. They can help you with emotions ranging from feeling lonely to being upset, angry and annoyed. Tell someone what's wrong at the time. If you wait until later in your life it can build up and fester. This is not good for you or your health.

**TIP!**

**Louise Hay has a brilliant book called *You Can Heal Your Life* which explains how many illnesses have other root causes – fascinating stuff.**

If you are a single parent or you have suffered the loss of a partner, husband or wife, it's difficult, no doubt. The angels applaud you for managing and doing your best. At the same time, they don't want you to feel lonely. Help and connection with friends really is for the taking, you just need to look in the right place! It will come, step-by-step. Keep smiling on your journey, even when you don't feel like it. There's always something to smile about, from a loving hug you received today, to enjoying a delicious breakfast, that morning cup of tea or coffee or seeing some blossoming flowers in a vase or a garden. Look for something to smile about and you will find it. The angels will help you to see.

For those who are bereaved, recently or a long time ago, it's difficult to carry on alone without a special person, especially when you did everything together and lived together for so long, but the angels don't want you to feel lonely. Their presence and unconditional love will be there for you. The thing is, as hard as this may sound, when someone's passed over, they are instantly at peace and they aren't grieving at all. They are happy, which might sound harsh, but they want you to feel happy too. They want you to remember the happy memories and they are always sorry (if there's something they need to say sorry for) in their crossing over to heaven or whatever you want to call it! They love to leave you signs such as feathers and coins to let you know they're still around and love you. You really are never alone. Your guardian angel is there by your side but equally your loved ones are there too. Knowing this, your sadness can eventually dissolve into peace, peace can dissolve into happiness, happiness can dissolve into tears and the deep emotions you have for your loved one. The love will never dissolve.

When you're going through hard times, for example, an illness, attending hospital appointments, or worrying about staying in hospital can feel quite lonely at times when you want someone to be there for you. This might be to hold your hand, keep you company or just have someone to talk to. You can ask a friend or family member to be with you or to help – people love to help! Sometimes we just have to pluck up the courage to ask. If this is not possible, always remember you can ask your guardian angel to help as well. It's not that you can't talk to your guardian angel, because you have discovered by reading this book that you can! And they will respond. If you need to go away or holiday on your own, or have a stay in hospital, make sure you take your favourite angel cards and books with you. You could also pack some of your favourite things from your angel altar. Tuck them in your bag and use them when you need to.

Knowing you are not alone is so comforting,

There might be other times of stress, or even severe stress in your life. Don't hesitate to ask a trusted friend or family member to support you with the more practical things you need help with. At the same time you can ask for help from your angels as well as being comforted by some of your favourite things like lavender essential oil and candles for calm and relaxation. A combination of remedies, practical help from trusted family and friends, and support from your angels, as well as your favourite things and activities can help lift your spirits and help you to cope.

## How you can help yourself during stressful times

If you don't have a best friend on hand to always talk to, you can be your own best friend. It is so easy to be harsh on ourselves and we have all experienced that inner voice that is critical and sometimes mean about ourselves, our actions and behaviours. Instead, we should speak to ourselves as a best friend. We should be kind, patient and more forgiving of ourselves. Author Cheryl Richardson says it helps to speak to yourself like a lovely best friend or like you would to a five-year-old child. You wouldn't dream of talking to a child in a horrid voice. Talk to yourself in a kind, loving way as if you were still little. Next time you hear that voice in your head being mean to you, try it!

Having a pet is a truly wonderful way to bring

more company into your life. If it isn't always possible to have a pet, you can still enjoy friends' or family members' pets or, when you're out on a walk say hello and stroke that lovely dog!

Your guardian angel would also like you to be aware that nature is part of your support network as well. The trees, the birds, the wildlife; perhaps your garden or a balcony with flowers. Even in your home you can bring that support in with live plants such as peace lilies and fresh flowers.

**TIP!**

**It's well known in Feng Shui that this is good for both your home and you, according to authors like Davina MacKail and Patricia Lohan.**

Plants and flowers can give you that wonder that is the miracle of life – how things grow and how you can constantly grow and evolve as a person too.

Here are some exercises for you to share with your angels. Each exercise will help you find ways to fill your days with happiness and take away those lonely feelings.

**TIP!**

**Make sure you include your angels in these and ask them for their help and guidance.**

**Your angel 'feel-good' jar**

How do you lift your mood when you are having a lonely day? A brilliant thing to have to hand is an angel 'feel-good' jar. The jar helps you to pick something relaxing or fun to do as guided by your angel.

**How to make an angel feel-good jar**

**What you need:**

⟫ An empty clean jar (with the lid, if you still have it)

⟫ Pen, pencil, colouring pens or even glitter pens!

**TIP!**

**Borrow these from your children or grandchildren or treat yourself to some sparkly stationery.**

⟫ Glue or tape

⟫ Paper or card. You can recycle birthday cards. You can use patterned card or create your own designs

⟫ Scissors.

**Before you begin your crafty creation, say this prayer:**

*Guardian angel, please surround me with your unconditional love; shine your bright light on me for guidance, for positivity, healing, happiness and inspiration. Let your light shine on me like the sun, in my life and my work. Guardian angel, please help me to talk to you and to receive your guidance and love with creating my feel-good jar.*
*With gratitude, I thank you.*

Place your hands on your heart. Close your eyes and take five relaxing breaths in and out before you start. Breathe in through your nose and breathe out through your mouth, relaxing on each out breath.
Then begin:

- Decorate your jar with words that make you feel good and anything else you feel inspired to draw, colour or write.

- Cut up small pieces of paper or card.

- Write down different things that you can do and that make you feel good and place each one in your jar.

**IDEAS to write down on the paper in your angel feel-good jar**

💡 Candlelit bath

💡 Sleep by 10pm, get 7-9 hours' sleep a night

💡 Choose a meditation

💡 Candlelit yoga or pilates

💡 Phone off by 7.30pm

💡 Have a laugh with someone

💡 Put on your favourite music and sing loudly

💡 Go to a sauna

💡 Go for a favourite walk

💡 Use Positive affirmations

💡 Pick an angel card and give yourself permission to do what it says

💡 Bounce on a rebounder or dance to a brilliant song

💡 Space clearing in your home

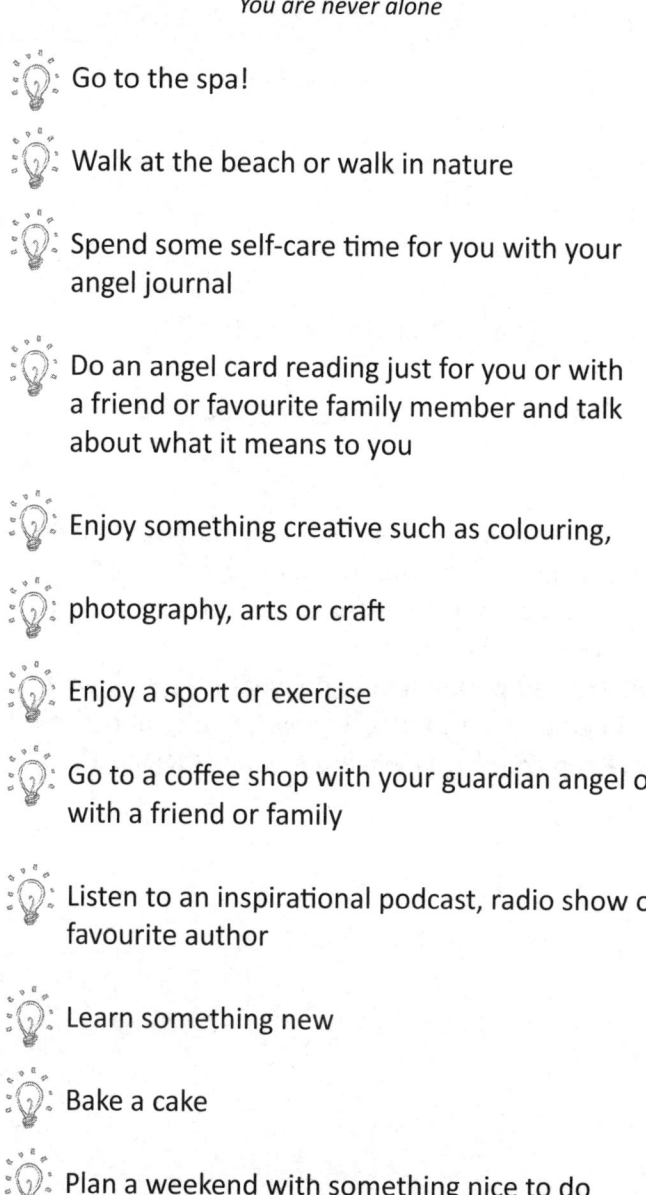

💡 Go to the spa!

💡 Walk at the beach or walk in nature

💡 Spend some self-care time for you with your angel journal

💡 Do an angel card reading just for you or with a friend or favourite family member and talk about what it means to you

💡 Enjoy something creative such as colouring,

💡 photography, arts or craft

💡 Enjoy a sport or exercise

💡 Go to a coffee shop with your guardian angel or with a friend or family

💡 Listen to an inspirational podcast, radio show or favourite author

💡 Learn something new

💡 Bake a cake

💡 Plan a weekend with something nice to do

💡 Eat something delicious

💡 Watch a favourite or new film

💡 Play or have fun with your child or pet

💡 Play a card or board game

💡 Take a nap in the day – and why not!

💡 Take time out to read your favourite book.

When you are in need of guidance and inspiration or you just want to lift your mood for the day, find your jar, take off the lid and ask your guardian angel to help you pick from the jar.
Give yourself permission to do what it says. Then if you need or want to feel even better, pick another one. Keep going until you are feeling FANTASTIC!

# Mindful colouring with your guardian angel

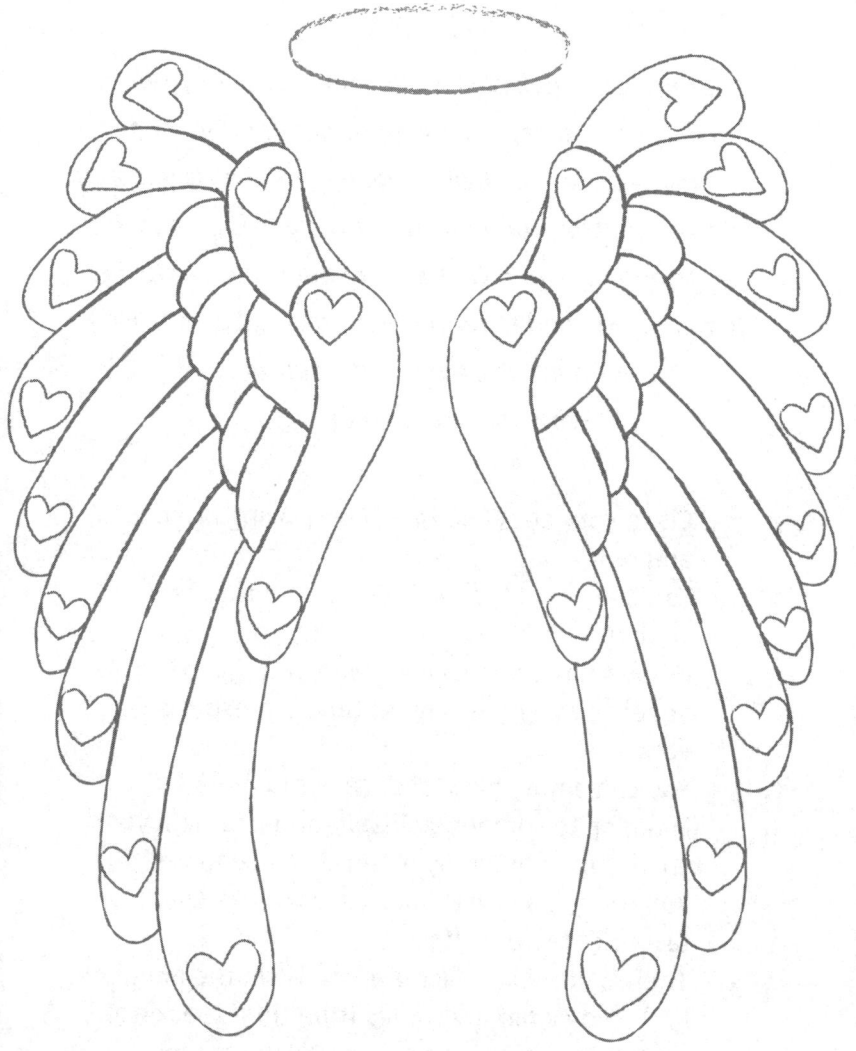

**Say your angel prayer:**

*Guardian angel, please surround me with your
unconditional love; shine your bright light on me for
guidance, for positivity, healing, happiness and
inspiration. Let your light shine on me like the sun, in
my life and my work. Guardian angel, please help me
to talk to you and to receive your guidance and love
with my creativity and colouring.*
*With gratitude, I thank you.*

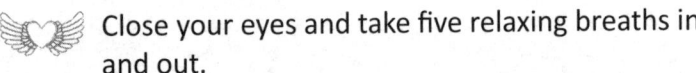 Close your eyes and take five relaxing breaths in
and out.

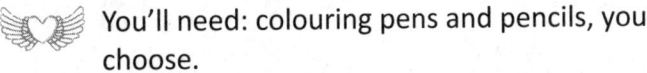 You'll need: colouring pens and pencils, you
choose.

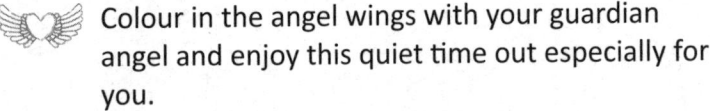 Colour in the angel wings with your guardian
angel and enjoy this quiet time out especially for
you.

You can enjoy this in silence, with music,
listening to something inspirational or with your
child, friend or family member, you choose.

You can get a nice drink such as herbal tea, or a
favourite tea or coffee.

There's nothing to achieve but be in the moment
and enjoy what joy comes from the experience
or draw or paint your own angel wings; get
creative.

**TIP!**

**Why not colour in other images or doodle on the pages in this book too?**

Although your guardian angel is with you all of the time, you can decide when you want to ask for help or spend quality time together. Their presence is like a present, a gift you can call upon at any moment – it doesn't have to be your birthday or Christmas day!

At the same time, being sociable with others is very important and will keep the feelings of loneliness at bay and make you feel more included in your community. Your guardian angel will encourage you to be sociable.

When you are feeling in a dark or solitary place the best thing to do is ask your guardian angel for help – however hard it may be at the time, make sure you do something about it.

**TIP!**

**Make sure you have meaningful interactions with others on a daily basis, whether it's chatting with someone at the post office or supermarket, a short phone call with friends or family or stopping to pat a dog and talk to its owner when out walking.**

Make sure you go out as often as you can and remember your guardian angel is always with you to keep you company. Enjoy being with them as much as they enjoy being with you.

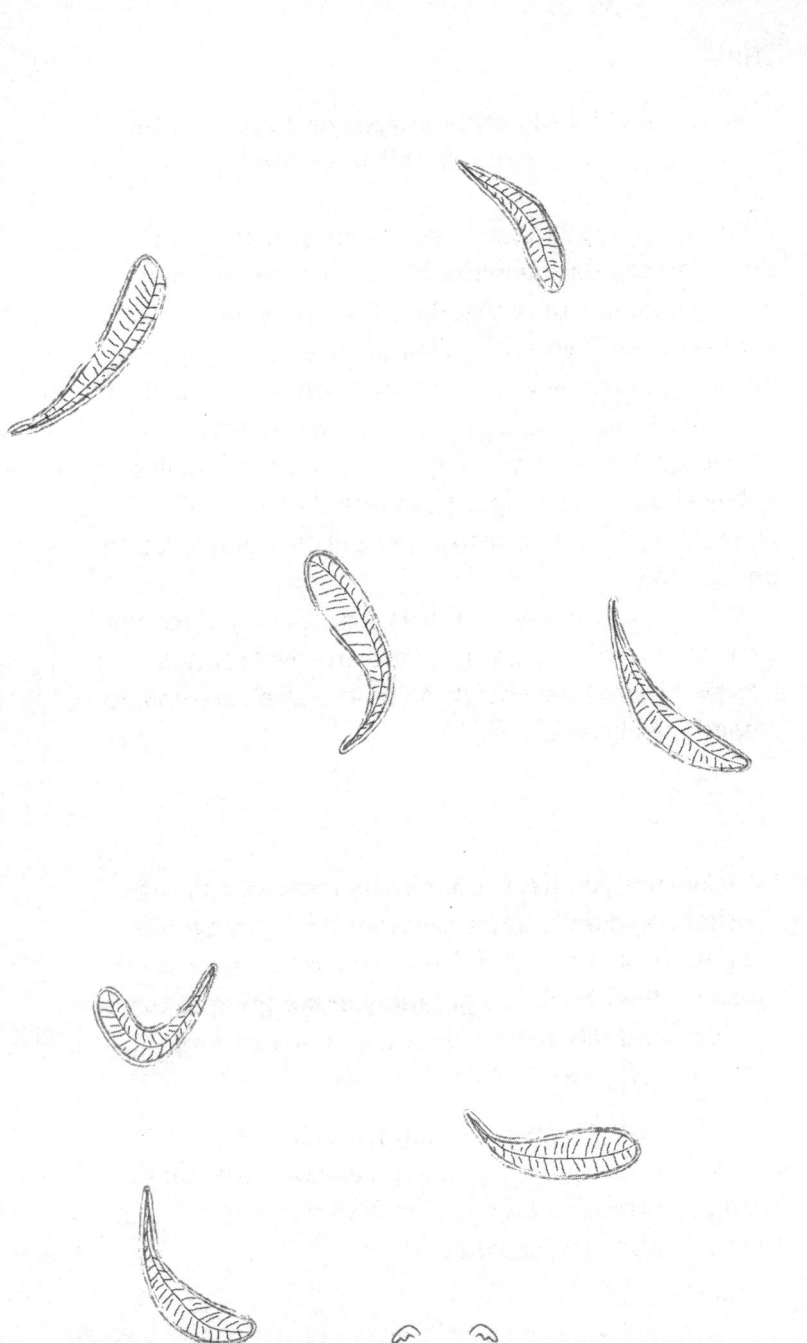

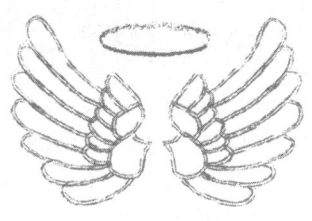

## Chapter 8

*"To err is human, to forgive, divine."*
**Alexander Pope**

*"True forgiveness is when you can say, "Thank you for that experience."*
**Oprah Winfrey**

**Forgiveness**

The angels so want to help you with forgiveness. But what exactly is forgiveness? The Oxford Dictionary definition of forgiveness is to 'stop feeling angry or resentful towards (someone) for an offence, flaw, or mistake.'

You may think this is easier said than done, and yes, sometimes it is. The angels have a few tips and tricks to help you feel better. They can't stop you feeling the pain that has been caused but they can help you to feel less pain and to feel better as quickly as possible.

What your angels do want for you is to help you come to a place of forgiveness and peace in your heart at some point. If you let it eat away at you, your confidence and zest for life will no doubt wither.

It could be that someone has just made some

bitchy remarks towards you, or you feel you are being bullied. It might be to do with a behaviour you've seen someone do which feels awful to witness. Rest assured you can do something about it.

**TIP!** **If you don't address these issues you may find yourself getting bogged down in a cycle that is upsetting, which may not only lead to mental and emotional stress but may also lead you to feel physically ill as well.**

Let's begin with addressing anything like this that is bothering us and get if off our chests.

**Six steps to getting things off your chest**
**Step 1:** Say your angel prayer:

*Guardian angel, please surround me with your unconditional love; shine your bright light on me for guidance, for positivity, healing, happiness and inspiration. Let your light shine on me like the sun, in my life and my work. Guardian angel, please help me to talk to you and to receive your guidance and love and what messages you need me to know to get things off my chest.*
*With gratitude, I thank you.*

**Step 2:** Say:

> *It's OK for me to talk about how I feel.*
> *It's OK for me to ask for help.*
> *It's OK because my guardian angel is always by my side.*

**Step 3:** Time to get everything off your chest.
Write a letter to your guardian angel. It's OK to have a rant and be upset and angry when you do this. Let your emotions out and write about everything that is bothering you. Let it be raw and honest. You could be writing about someone you want to forgive. List all the things that are bothering you about what they have done. This is about helping you to own up to these feelings and helping you find a way to feel better.

**Step 4:** Once you've done this take a few moments to think about it and how much better you feel by admitting these feelings and getting them out of your head and off your chest. These feeling are now only angry words on the paper. Enjoy how good it feels to have released them.

**Step 5:** Now it's time to shred, burn or drown your letter before anyone else sees it. To drown it means getting a bowl of water and simply squidging the piece of paper in your hands until the ink runs. This act will give you freedom and permission to be released from all those bad feelings. This will give you the courage to forgive.

**Step 6:** Now we have released the bad feelings we are in a much better position to start taking steps to finding solutions. Write down the positive actions you can take.

If your letter was about being angry at someone and trying to forgive them, you could write down positive ways in which you can rebuild your relationship with them. However, note that this does not mean that you condone this person's behaviour at all. And you don't have to spend any more time with this person, people or situation if you don't want to. You can walk away.

**Please note: If you have experienced extreme upset from someone else's behaviour, although the angels are part of your support team you sometimes need to seek extra help, depending on the severity of the action, offence, flaw or mistake, and how much it's affected you and your family. In severe cases always speak to the correct professional whether this is the police, Social Services, your doctor, the Samaritans or other specialists that can help you.**

If you have decided that the best positive action after you have found forgiveness is to walk away from a person/s who have caused you hurt and pain, you will need to learn how to cut the cords. Invisible cords (or etheric cords) can attach between you and another person, created by a situation where there has been stress, anger and upset. They are like ropes, chains or cobwebs that bind you to them. You will feel them or sense them. They can have a real, detrimental effect on your well-being in lots of different ways. You may sense them, feel them, see them or simply 'know' they are there. A big reason they remain is because of a lack of forgiveness and the fact that the person still upsets you or stresses you out, even if they've passed away and are in heaven now. It can be a vicious cycle of stress that can perpetuate a level of low confidence in certain areas of your life and work, and even create a lack of romantic relationships especially if you've not yet got over your ex-partner. The good news is that you can free yourself of these cords. It's a great exercise for spring cleaning your aura too! I will show you how in the next exercise.

**Guardian angel cutting the cords and healing meditation**

Say your angel prayer:

*Guardian angel, please surround me with your unconditional love; shine your bright light on me for guidance, for positivity, healing, happiness and inspiration. Let your light shine on me like the sun, in my life and my work. Guardian angel, please help me to talk to you and to receive your guidance and love with cutting the cords meditation.*
*With gratitude, I thank you.*

> *Close your eyes and take five relaxing breaths in and out, breathing in through your nose, out through your mouth, relaxing more and more on each out breath.*

*Ask your guardian angel to help you cut the cords that are causing you stress. Imagine yourself breaking free.*

*Take a deep breath in and as you breathe out give yourself permission to cut these cords, allowing them to evaporate into love with the help of the angels. Allow these areas to be filled with love and healing, knowing that you are safe and protected and that you can move on knowing that you don't have to live with that stress anymore. It's over, it's in the past and now you can give yourself permission to live in the present, enjoying each moment as much as possible.*

*Picture the cords turning into ribbons as a celebration that it's over; smile that it's over. Watch the ribbons float away and disappear, knowing deep in your soul that you are now stronger for releasing yourself from this. Time for a fresh start, right here and right now.*

To finish this chapter here's a lovely feel good meditation that takes you through the colours of the rainbow.

**The rainbow angel meditation**

Breathe and relax. Welcome to the rainbow angel meditation.

Say your angel prayer:

*Guardian angel, please surround me with your unconditional love; shine your bright light on me for guidance, for positivity, healing, happiness and inspiration. Let your light shine on me like the sun, in my life and my work. Guardian angel, please help me to talk to you and to receive your guidance and love with this meditation.*

*With gratitude, I thank you.*

Close your eyes and take five relaxing breaths in and out, breathing in through your nose and out through your mouth, relaxing more and more on each out breath. Breathe in to your tummy; this abdominal breathing helps you keep your neck and shoulders relaxed and calm throughout. Imagine your tummy is inflating like a balloon inflating, and then let your tummy relax completely, soft and relaxed.

Picture the colours of the rainbow surrounding you now in a cloak and bubbles of colourful light and say to yourself "*I am safe*". Picture the colour red of a red rose surrounding you, the colour orange of a Satsuma surrounding you, picture the colour of a yellow daffodil surrounding you, the colour of your favourite plant or tree – a deep vibrant green – surrounding you, and the colour of a pale blue beautiful sky surrounding you. Now picture a deep blue-sky colour surrounding you in this incredible colour and finally picture the beautiful purple of an amethyst crystal surrounding you. Lucky you.

Say aloud the following. "*My heart and soul are protected always, with the colours of all of my favourite flowers and plants, meadows, nature and trees! My guardian angel guides and protects me always. I ask for help and I receive help. I give and I receive. It's safe for me to love, it's safe for me to be happy, it's safe for me to enjoy everything. I am grateful. I am truly blessed.*"

"*I picture the colour of the red rose and I am open to receiving more and more financial success and financial stability, I have the ability to save effortlessly and to enjoy being debt free, I am safe, I have very strong foundations and am so grateful for this.*"

"*I picture the colour orange, a tangerine colour surrounding me again. Its colour flows in like a superpower to cleanse my tummy. It's safe for me to enjoy the pleasure of my sexuality and have a love of pleasure.*"

Breathe. Relax.

"*I picture the colour of the yellow sun, daffodils or the daisy flower knowing that I am provided for. I see the colours of a citrine yellow crystal, this is a more golden yellow, like the rays of the sun streaming in. I have a feeling of safety and that I am safe. I cut the cords to me and any current or past stress and I give my guardian angel permission to do this for me and leave the cords of love behind so that I can move on, smile and be free to be me in every single way, both at home and work. Thank you. I do something fun every single day. I give myself this goal, no matter what's going on in my life: to do something fun, to laugh and to smile every single day. I smile when the sun is shining. I smile when I gaze at the yellow daffodils."*

Picture the colour green surrounding you, the colour of your favourite plant or tree – a deep vibrant green – surrounding you. Allow your heart to melt and be as happy right now as one of your favourite moments in your life. Remember that happy memory right now and allow that joy to soar into your heart. You deserve this.

Now picture the colour of a beautiful pale blue sky surrounding you, and remember a memory of when you were at your happiest speaking your truth, at your happiest in a particular situation expressing yourself. Firstly, think of a happy memory of when you were laughing and smiling on an outing or with friends or a favourite family member. Allow yourself to enjoy this memory of how you were loved and accepted just the way you are and how you expressed yourself easily and effortlessly in this situation because you felt so loved and at home. Pause, breathe and relax to enjoy this memory for a little longer.

Now picture a deep blue sky colour surrounding you in this incredible colour and allow yourself to remember a moment, a happy memory when you were able to see clearly in your life. This may be seeing your first angel feather, or it may be a happy memory of reading an amazing book, listening to an inspirational meditation or doing a spiritual or personal development course or training for the first time. Whatever it is, allow it to come in to inspire you to do more of this in your life. This is the seat of your intuition and the angels applaud you for this memory and for your ability to bring in more and more in this lifetime; how truly wonderful is that? Breathe and relax.

Finally, picture the beautiful purple of an amethyst crystal surrounding you. The crystal is so huge that you realise it's a beach hut made of amethyst surrounded by all of these amazing bluebells and hyacinths – and the scent of the flowers is just incredible. The healing properties of the beach hut help you feel so at peace, calm, happy and serene that you are keen to return. This is your connection to the universal source of love available to you at any time, and you may feel a tickle on your head, nose or face to show you that your guardian angel is with you at this very moment, cheering you on, guiding you, helping make their presence known to you.

This is a chance for you to tap into the wisdom of your wise soul. You need the time and space to understand how you communicate with your guardian angel – and they are there to show you how. Hang out with the angels more and invite them to join you at different times throughout the day. Incorporating them into your daily lifestyle will be one of the best investments you will ever make!

Sometimes you can feel spaced out after a meditation, especially in the head area as this is the area that you will become most connected to the wisdom and guidance from the angels. Rest assured that all you have to do is stay human too, and as a human get grounded afterwards and every day. This means get some fresh air, and connect to the earth too, for example by walking barefoot after meditation, opening the windows, going for a walk or having a glass of water or cup of tea. Take a deep breath in now and yawn. Relax.

It's now time to see yourself sit at the end of the rainbow. You look up at its beauty with awe and as you glance down you see your guardian angel really vividly in front of you. She is so beautiful; she's beaming at you with a huge rainbow aura – there are rainbows everywhere, and you have a rainbow aura too. You're all matching with rainbow auras and you laugh together at this fact! There's a treasure chest sitting next to you with pots of gold inside and it's shimmering, allowing you to see all the abundance in your life and all of the abundance that's waiting to come into your life. Make a wish, and let your wish fly up into the sky like a beautiful bird filled with love. Your guardian angel hands you a personal message. You accept it with gratitude.

*I am as free as a bird to do whatever I want with my life.*

Now spend some time with your angel journal and write your thoughts about what the personal message from your angel was here.

**Journal with your Angel**

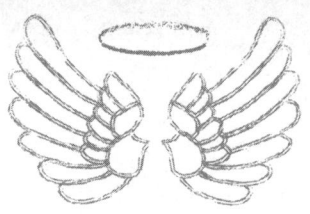

## Chapter 9

*"When I started counting my blessings,* my whole life turned around."

**Willie Nelson**

### Gratitude

Angels absolutely love an attitude with gratitude, and this is a fact!

They are big fans of what expressing gratitude can do for you and your life. You may be doing it already in lots of ways, but the exciting thing is you can always take it to the next level – and the angels love to help you with this. The more you spend time with your guardian angel the more gratitude you will experience. Your mindset will shift to more of a growth mindset about what you believe you can do and achieve.

Psychologist Dr Carol Dweck, in her book *Mindset*, talks about how your mindset can help you fulfil your potential. Carol Dweck's research advocates the power of praising effort as opposed to an achievement. Although it's wonderful that Serena Williams has won Wimbledon many times, to praise her only on the achievement will not help her with her growth mindset. Being praised for the improvement and effort will. This praise reaps huge dividends to us all in both childhood and adulthood. This praise encourages the love of and gratitude for learning.

Matthew Syed talks about the power of practice and how that creates improvement in what you want to get better at. This results in building confidence, self-esteem and effectively your gratitude for what you're improving and enjoying. It's exciting stuff and you can experience this too!

Let's practice being grateful for the simple pleasures in life.

 Walk around your home and give thanks for all the things you love in your home and your life, and as you wander talk to your angels and say *"Thank you for…"* (List whatever you love here). It could be the purple tulips in the vase, for the yellow daffodils, for the abundance of food and drink in your kitchen. If you live with someone, think of one thing about them that you are grateful for, then two things, then three and let the list go on and on. Depending on how much time you have you can try out this gratitude exercise daily with the angels to supercharge your gratitude and happiness.

 Make a list of the things that came to mind and **journal with the angels** here:

I am grateful for….

**TIP!**

**Think about happy memories of wonderful times you've spent with your parents, friends or children. It may have encouraged you to gaze at the colour of the fresh flowers and smell their scent, it may have given you a moment to acknowledge the hard work you've put in with a work project and say well done for that effort. You may have been invited to a wedding of a friend or family and it's an opportunity when you see that invitation sitting there to look forward to it and give gratitude for the invitation and perhaps start planning your outfit!**

Now, let's hot things up a little and get our bodies moving! Here's a great feel-good exercise that works every time.

**Dancing gratitude with your angel**
**For one minute, two minutes or five – 'set a timer!'**

Say your angel prayer:

*Guardian angel, please surround me with your unconditional love; shine your bright light on me for guidance, for positivity, healing, happiness and inspiration. Let your light shine on me like the sun, in my life and my work. Guardian angel, please help me to talk to you and to receive your guidance and love when I'm dancing.*
*With gratitude, I thank you.*

 Close your eyes and take five relaxing breaths in and out, breathing in through your nose and out through your mouth, relaxing more and more on each out breath. Breathe in to your tummy; this abdominal breathing helps you keep your neck and shoulders relaxed and calm throughout. Imagine your tummy is inflating like a balloon inflating, and then let your tummy relax completely, soft and relaxed. You can do this sitting, standing or lying down depending on how much time you have and want to spend on this!) Whichever feels right to you.

 Then press play on an uplifting song or playlist and off you go! Dance around the room – be as lively as you can and have fun! If you can, dance from room to room being grateful for everything in each room.

 Talk to your angels and say:

*Thank you for* ............... as you DANCE and SMILE, as it conjures up gratitude after gratitude.
*Thank you for*.............. (you fill in the blanks).
It may be about fresh flowers, food, who you live with if you live with your family or pet, or it might be about physical objects such as your favourite essential oil burner or comfy bed. It might be about how much you appreciate someone making you breakfast that day; it can be anything.

 Dance until the music track finishes. You can always play it again or choose another track!

If you are restricted to sitting in a chair, move as many body parts as you can, laugh and have fun! You might love having your arms in the air, swaying your arms from side to side like you're at a music concert! Or tapping your feet side to side or jumping up and down for the catchy bits. You decide how you dance! Your way is the best!

Enjoy the magic that dancing brings to your mood, energy levels, vitality and happiness. See your gratitude increase for all the things you have to be grateful for in your life. Friends or family may have made or bought you lovely gifts, you may have some happy memories dotted around with photos of some of your favourite experiences or places that also you'd love to go to again; you may have positive affirmations around that you love reading and absorbing on a daily basis such as an inspirational calendar too. The list is endless.

**TIP!** **Make sure that you take regular breaks if you're doing computer type work or anything that requires you to sit still and concentrate. Get up and dance with your angels and see what a difference this makes!**

Now we are going to calm things down and relax and allow ourselves time to daydream.

## Angel gratitude daydreaming meditation

Make yourself comfy; you may be sitting or lying down. Perhaps tuck yourself up in a cosy warm blanket.

Say your angel prayer:

*Guardian angel, please surround me with your unconditional love; shine your bright light on me for guidance, for positivity, healing, happiness and inspiration. Let your light shine on me like the sun, in my life and my work. Guardian angel, please help me to talk to you and to receive your guidance and love when daydreaming.*
*With gratitude, I thank you.*

Close your eyes and take five relaxing breaths in and out, breathing in through your nose and out through your mouth, relaxing more and more on each out breath. Breathe in to your tummy; this relaxed, abdominal breathing helps you keep your neck and shoulders relaxed and calm throughout. Imagine your tummy is inflating like a balloon inflating, and then let your tummy relax completely, soft and relaxed.

As you sit or lie down all cosy and quiet, enjoy this sacred and special time with your guardian angel to count your blessings, one at a time, as you daydream about everything or just some of the things you're grateful for right now in your life and work. Think of anything that you're grateful for right now and say to your guardian angel, *"Thank you for..."* (whatever it is). As you go through your day, say to your guardian angel, *"Thank you for..."* (you get the joy of filling in the blanks). From the moment you wake up to the time you go to sleep the angels are a big fan of counting your blessings as you go about your day. Your attitude and thoughts will no doubt shape your day. Picture your day ahead and give thanks for your bed and sleep, look forward to some wonderful self-care time for you, look forward to the delicious, nutritious meals you are going to eat, and enjoy the thoughts of how you would love your day to go, whether it's a work and play day or a day off. You get to decide how you want it to go with your attitude of gratitude. Just for today, be calm; just for today, be hopeful and have dreams and goals; just for today, be grateful; just for today, be kind; just for today enjoy everything you possibly can and surround everything with a hug from your guardian angel, knowing that everyone else has one they can call upon too.

 What do you want to get done today? What fun do you want to have? What joy do you want to bring to yourself? What joy do you want to bring to your home, friends, family, relationships, or even food? Perhaps you're about to try a new recipe and you're feeling gratitude for that.

> Breathe in through your nose, exhale through your mouth, and relax.

 Daydream about what you'd love to bring into your day to feel even more gratitude today. It may be a blissful walk in nature to get some exercise, or enjoying essential oils such as lavender on your pillow to help you relax even more deeply in meditation and sleep better at bedtime.

 Daydream about how you want it to go with your family and friends today, whether you're going to do something fun together like an outing or to enjoy a happy dinner together. Whatever it is, thank your guardian angel for this. Allow yourself to receive your angel's guidance.

> Breathe and relax; breathe in through your nose and out through your mouth.

 Is there anything arty you would love to do today, like colour something in, write nicely or design something or learn something artistic or simply enjoy someone else's art in some way? What do you feel inspired to watch or listen to today? Is it a Ted talk, inspirational interview, podcast or personal and spiritual development audio or audiobook? Perhaps make the mundane inspirational with music or one of these ideas. Breathe and relax. The angels applaud you for taking this time for rest and relaxation right now. Is there anything else you'd like to do today to help you rest and relax? Give gratitude for making this a priority. The angels are clapping yet again. In a very growth mindset way, say thank you and well done for taking this time for your rest and relaxation as it's as important as anything else. You deserve this time for you – you'll feel better and everyone else will reap the rewards when you are rested. Well done for taking this time to rest and recharge. The angels are grateful you did.

> Breathe and relax. Breathe in through your nose and out through your mouth. Relax.

What do you love? Who do you love? What and who inspires you? Do more of that. Then it's easier and easier to feel and receive more and more gratitude in your life and more and more thankful moments to treasure. You are treasured by your guardian angel, never forget that.

**Journal with your guardian angel**

Invite your angel to journal with you as you ask these questions:

  What brings me joy in my life?

♡ What am I feeling hugely grateful for right now?

♡ Who could I write a hand-written note, card or letter to, to express my gratitude and thanks to them?

♡ What are my favourite things about my work? Say thank you for the things you enjoy about this.

♡ What are those little precious things that you feel immensely grateful for such as a hug or little quirks and affectionate moments you have with your family or friends?

♡ What's one of your favourite drinks? Give thanks for this!

♡ What's one of your favourite foods or meals? Say thank you!

♡ What's one of your favourite meditations? Give yourself permission to do it more! And say thank you!

♡ Where do you love to go in nature? Go more. Say thank you for this wonderful place that recharges your soul

♡ Where do you love to walk? Go more! Give thanks.

♡ What makes you laugh and smile? Do it more, much more. Say thank you every single time you smile, laugh and giggle.

**TIP!** **Writing your gratitude down can be hugely therapeutic and uplifting and help you focus on what is going really well in your life and what you're enjoying, loving and grateful for, allowing more of this to flow in.**

Why not create your very own thank you jar? This is similar to our feel-good jar but this time we are putting things in it! Talk to your angels and ask them to help you.

This is a wonderful exercise that will have a positive effect on so many things and it's something that's enjoyable to do every day. You can also give thanks for things that haven't yet come into fruition that you want to manifest. Visualise what you want to happen and be grateful for it.

**How to create an angel thank you jar**
Say your angel prayer:

*Guardian angel, please surround me with your unconditional love; shine your bright light on me for guidance, for positivity, healing, happiness and inspiration. Let your light shine on me like the sun, in my life and my work. Guardian angel, please help me to talk to you and to receive your guidance and love with creating my thank you jar.*
*With gratitude, I thank you.*

Close your eyes and take five relaxing breaths in and out, breathing in through your nose and out through your mouth, relaxing more and more on each out breath. Breathe in to your tummy; this abdominal breathing helps you keep your neck and shoulders relaxed and calm throughout. Imagine your tummy is inflating like a balloon inflating, and then let your tummy relax completely, soft and relaxed. Do this sitting, wherever inspires you, whether it's out in nature, cosy tucked up in bed or on a favourite sofa, armchair, beanbag or chair!

 Open your eyes.

**What you need:**

- An empty jar
- Pen
- Paper
- Scissors
- Colouring pens and pencils and anything else you would like to have for your thank you jar

You may like to have magazines to cut up too in case you feel inspired to cut out things that you're wanting to bring into your life.

 Decorate your jar! Get as creative as you like and stick on whatever you feel inspired to use.

 The first time you do your jar, think of at least ten things you're thankful for and cut out individual pieces of paper for each one, write it out and post it in the jar (if you want to you can write the date on the back).

If you're inspired to write out things that you're wanting to bring into your life then write: *"Angels I thank you for..."* (you fill in the blank), or simply cut out a picture of what you're wanting to bring in or words from a magazine. It might be more peace, meditation, or a specific item of clothing, a holiday, work success or a new experience. You choose.

At the end, hold your jar and take five breaths in and out, breathing in through your nose and out through your mouth. Think of everything you have placed in the jar that you are thankful for. Thank your guardian angel for their help.

You can add more to your jar daily or on a regular basis. This can be a wonderful family activity where each member talks about and adds their thank you cards to the jar. It is a way to bring happiness and share good memories with your family.

### Take a negative news break

You will love this idea if you find yourself surrounded with negativity, situations or news that makes you feel down, moody, stressed or low in any way. The thing is, there's a lot going on in the world. If you find yourself reading the newspapers, watching the news and talking about the bad news then you can choose to stop! You can take a negative news break. This means that for one to seven days you make the decision to take certain negative things out of your life. You may decide to not watch the news or talk about the news, or not read the newspaper, or to avoid the internet or the social media negativity that is so rife these days. You have the choice to take a break!

With the help of your angels, when you catch yourself wanting to have a good old moan, instead think of something you can be grateful for – do one of the meditations or read your affirmations or use your feel-good jar. Talk to your family and friends about only positive and happy things. Become a solution-focused friend. Someone that people love to have around. Your angel will only ever offer you positive and uplifting messages. Why not be the same?

Talk to your guardian angel and ask for their help.

Say your angel prayer:

*Guardian angel, please surround me with your unconditional love; shine your bright light on me for guidance, for positivity, healing, happiness and inspiration. Let your light shine on me like the sun, in my life and my work. Guardian angel, please help me to talk to you and to receive your guidance and love with removing the negative things in my life and taking a break from these.*
*With gratitude, I thank you.*

Close your eyes and take five relaxing breaths in and out, breathing in through your nose and out through your mouth, relaxing more and more on each out breath. Breathe in to your tummy; this abdominal breathing helps you keep your neck and shoulders relaxed and calm throughout. Imagine your tummy is inflating like a balloon inflating, and then let your tummy relax completely, soft and relaxed. Do this sitting, wherever inspires you – whether it's out in nature, cosy tucked up in bed or on a favourite sofa, armchair, beanbag or chair!

 Open your eyes.

Say: *I can choose to take a negative news break if I want. I'm going to be optimistic and choose one gratitude exercise or meditation to do every day. When I feel negative, I'm going to talk to my angels and take a break from people who are negative, stressful or start talking about bad news. I will walk away politely. I give myself permission to take a break from newspapers and the news. I enjoy having an attitude of gratitude and will talk to myself and others with kindness, love and respect with gratitude for every single encounter I have at home and work.*

See how you go; say this every single morning and before you go to sleep at night, and see what a difference it makes in one week.

**TIP!**

**Remember, we are not perfect so anytime you slip up then just say sorry to yourself, forgive yourself, tell yourself "I love you", ask your angel for strength and guidance and start again! It's as easy as that.**

The angels are grateful for your willingness to bring more gratitude into your life and know you will be glad you did.

### Gratitude affirmations with your guardian angel

Enjoy these affirmations anytime you'd like a little or big boost. Ask your guardian angel to cheer you on, saying them out loud or silently, or feel free to bounce on a re-bounder saying them or jump around the room singing them.

Talk to your guardian angel and say:

 *Thank you for my life.*

 *Thank you for smiling right now! (Smile with your angel).*

 *Thank you for my happiness.*

 *Thank you for my healing.*

 *Thank you for music.*

 *Thank you for singing my positive affirmations.*

 *Thank you for dancing with joy.*

 *Thank you for my home.*

 *Thank you for my lovely friends.*

 *Thank you for my wonderful work.*

 *Thank you for my health and well-being.*

 *Thank you for all the abundance in my life.*

 *Thank you for you being in my life.*

 *Thank you for your guidance.*

 *Thank you for your life and support.*

 *Thank you for angel cards and positive affirmation cards for daily guidance, I'm grateful.*

 *Thank you for showing me signs and loving me.*

 *Thank you for talking to me.*

*Thank you for giving me words of guidance, tips and re-assurance. I'm truly grateful.*

 *Thank you for giving me signs such as a feather to know I'm loved, supported and on the right path.*

 *Thank you for me noticing your messages through songs and words I think and overhear.*

 *Thank you for enabling me to feel your heavenly presence of angel tickles and angel hugs.*

 *Thank you for listening when I talk to you.*

 *I know I am always loved, guided and supported. For that I'm truly grateful.*

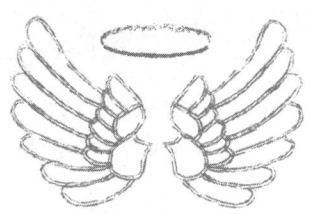

## Chapter 10

*"If life isn't about human beings and living in harmony,
then I don't know what it's about."*
**Orlando Bloom**

### Harmonious relationships

Isn't it wonderful when your relationships are going
really well and you get that warm fuzzy feeling of
unconditional love when being hugged? However,
humans are complicated and not everyone is always
nice to us all the time. So, what do we do? We talk to
our angels. They want to help us as much as possible
to enjoy our relationships and for us to be as happy
and loving as possible. This all starts with you, with
your relationship with yourself, how you speak to
yourself, the kindness you show yourself and of course
your thoughts and attitude towards yourself. You need
to learn how to practice self-love.

We can encourage ourselves to think more positive
thoughts – and of course it's about that magical word,
practice – practicing the better thoughts and calming
the not-so-good ones. By using the meditations and
affirmations in this book and with the help of your
angels you can learn to love yourself more.

There is evidence that through meditation we
can access a healing state. How interesting is that?

Perhaps one day hospitals will have meditation wards, healing wards and positive thinking wards. Now that would be interesting!

In the meantime, let's see what wisdom comes through from the angels. Starting with yourself means loving yourself just the way you are.

Here's a little exercise to get us going.

**The self-love heart flower angel colouring for guidance and inspiration**

This exercise is a self-love exercise to improve your relationship with yourself, to help you enjoy your own company more, love yourself even more and in turn improve your relationships with others. It can also be about making peace with those who have passed over. Say your angel prayer:

*Guardian angel, please surround me with your unconditional love; shine your bright light on me for guidance, for positivity, healing, happiness and inspiration. Let your light shine on me like the sun, in my life and my work. Guardian angel, please help me to talk to you and to receive your guidance and love with finding my own self-love and with my heart flower colouring exercise.*
*With gratitude, I thank you.*

Close your eyes and take five relaxing breaths in and out, breathing in through your nose and out through your mouth, relaxing more and more on each out breath. Breathe in to your tummy; this abdominal breathing helps you keep your neck and shoulders relaxed and calm throughout. Imagine your tummy is inflating like a balloon inflating, and then let your tummy relax completely, soft and relaxed. Do this sitting in your favourite chair, at a table or cosy tucked up in bed with something to lean on, or draw it straight into your angel journal. You choose.

**What you need:**

> Colouring pens

> Pencils

> Deck of your favourite angel cards or positive affirmation cards

Colour in each heart in a colour that calls to you, then write the following words in each heart which makes up the petals of the flower. The final two you can draw as heart shaped leaves with the stem.

♡ Health

♡ Self-care

♡ Abundance and money

♡ Home

♡ Leisure (hobbies and fun)

♡ Work

♡ Family and friends

♡ Personal and spiritual development

♡ Self-love and romance.

Write one or more things that you love about each area of your life.

Then ask your guardian angel this question. *What would you like me to know in this area of my life?* Then write what comes to you, and trust that it's divinely guided by your guardian angel. Enjoy the process and allow yourself to be guided by your guardian angel.

Then pick an angel card, a positive affirmation card and see what it says. Write it down here

_____

_____

Think about what that means to you in relation to that area of your life. Then once again ask your guardian angel to help you to receive their messages about the card too. Do as much as you're guided to do.

Make your notes here:

_____

_____

_____

_____

_____

_____

_____

**TIP!** **You can even enjoy this activity with a favourite friend or family member. What fun! Equally, you can get some brilliant guidance for your entire life, harmonious relationships and happiness, starting with your special heart flower self-love colouring. Enjoy.**

The key to harmonious relations is finding the harmony within yourself. The most important message so far in this chapter is that you need to learn to love yourself. You are better off being single and loving yourself than being in a relationship and not loving yourself.

If you are experiencing a relationship that doesn't feel right to you it could affect your confidence and you will stop feeling good about yourself. Think of a shark meeting a beautiful tropical fish; the tropical fish stands no chance of survival. In a human sense, being with the wrong person could swallow your heart and soul. This is not the path your guardian angel wants for you. Your path is harmony and to re–find harmony when things get out of balance.

Now this may surprise you, but four of the biggest factors that contribute to me having happy relationships, according to my guardian angel, are:

1. Getting enough sleep.
2. Being financially stable and knowing and feeling like I have enough money.
3. Being able to talk to my angel in some way, the easiest way being using the angel cards for as many of my relationship issues as possible.

4.  For me to have a romantic relationship it will always have to be kind and loving.

Ask your angels, what are the four biggest things to you having happy relationships?

**Journal with your angel here**

_____

_____

_____

_____

_____

_____

_____

_____

_____

_____

_____

**TIP!** **Author Julie New has a book called *Who are the Flowers in Your Garden?* describing relationships like a garden – you need to water them to flourish and equally, you need to water yourself so that you can flourish too. Such true and wise words, ones that everyone can learn from.**

What else can we do to help improve our relationships?

Often the simplest things work.

You may need help in a relationship as well as help bringing you both a more loving, kind connection, strengthening and deepening your relationship with your friend, family member, work colleague or children.

Your Angel Cards are the perfect way to bring people together. Try popping them in a jar or a special bowl so that friends enjoy picking one when they come over. You could scatter the cards around your home, stick them up on a wall, take them in the car, or pop them in your bag when you travel. Notice how your happiness and mood soar in a different way each day, as you bring more of this magic into your life.

**TIP!** **You can spread this joy further by being a gift angel and buying someone their very own sets of angel or positive affirmation cards, or including individual cards you post, such as for birthdays, or any correspondence where you want to pass on this incredible gift of love.**

Picking cards together with your angel is a wonderful way for you and others to express how you feel and this is so important. Make sure you invite your angels to join you. Talk to them. Having them present makes the space feel more positive than just having an ordinary conversation. Truly a gift of love at its best.

**How to do a loving angel card reading just for you:**

Ideally, create a relaxing ambience for your reading when you have extra time.

 Light a candle.

 Find a tidy, relaxing and comfortable space to do your reading (although if you prefer you can pick a card anywhere!)

 Say your angel prayer:

*Guardian angel, please surround me with your unconditional love; shine your bright light on me for guidance, for positivity, healing, happiness and inspiration. Let your light shine on me like the sun, in my life and my work. Guardian angel, please help me to talk to you and to receive your guidance and love with my angel card reading.*
*With gratitude, I thank you.*

Close your eyes and take five relaxing breaths in and out, breathing in through your nose and out through your mouth, relaxing more and more on each out breath. Breathe in to your tummy; this abdominal breathing helps you keep your neck and shoulders relaxed and calm throughout. Imagine your tummy is inflating like a balloon inflating, and then let your tummy relax completely, soft and relaxed. You can do this sitting, standing or lying down depending on how much time you have and want to spend on this! Whichever feels right to you.

 Tap the cards to put your vibration and energy into the cards and to clear any negativity or stress they may have absorbed. Make it your intention that the reading is positive and uplifting and will give you the guidance and answers you seek right now in your life. Set the intention for the reading, such as *Angel what guidance would you like me to know today?* Shuffle the cards.

 Ask your guardian angel to tell you when to stop shuffling. You may just know when to stop, or you may think the word *stop,* guiding you to stop shuffling. Or simply stop shuffling! Fan the cards out.

 Ask your guardian angel to guide you which card to pick. You may see the right card to pick, you may know which card to pick in a knowing, magnetic way, you feel a particular card is the right one, or you may receive guidance with all

of the above ways. You can never do an incorrect reading. The card you pick will always be the correct card for you.

Read what it says, and look at the picture if there's a picture.

Think to yourself, if it's not already obvious: 'What does this card message mean to me'?

Write down or think about what comes to you. Then ask your guardian angel, *Is there anything else you'd like to tell me with your guidance about this message? Thank you.* Write what comes to you from your guardian angel.

**TIP!** **The most common way your guardian angel will communicate with you is through claircognizance – clear thinking of knowing the words and thoughts that your angel is communicating with you. These are often the most helpful and powerful messages.**

So, you need to write down every single word that comes to you. You may get visions of what the angels want you to know, such as a photo or video image in your mind. The more you get to know your deck of angel cards, the more you will be able to visualise with them. You may even get a vision of a different angel card in the pack that doesn't exist! You may hear a song in your mind with the lyrics of the song giving you a special message. You may get tickles on your face from your angel as you read certain words. The angels may add extra words in, to give you what they want you to know. Remember, practice this. Practice will hone your skill at using the cards and this exercise will become very enjoyable.

Write your thoughts from this meditation here and journal with your guardian angel. Ask your guardian angel if there are any action steps to take, then make a list and plan to make it happen.

**Journal with your angel**

_____

_____

_____

_____

_____

_____

_____

_____

_____

_____

_____

_____

_____

**Here are some ideas for using your angel cards**
**Slide reading**

The slide reading is often a real favourite and shifts the energy in a fun and vibrant way. All you do is slide the cards along a table or floor, for example. Wheeeee! And off they go. Then pick the card that you're guided to pick. If you're guided to pick more than one card, do so.

**Got a question you need answering?**

Simple. Just ask your guardian angel the question whilst you are shuffling and then see what guidance comes up with the card message. Trust that the card message will be just what you need to receive right now. It might not be what you are expecting, and it might not be clear how that message answers your question. Keep following each crumb of guidance and they will add up to magical solutions to your questions. With the help of your angels you will get there in the end. Make sure you relax and enjoy the process. Remember, the angels will only want what's good for you and the messages will always be positive.

**The three card Past, Present and Future spread**

This can be a great way of getting extra information, so pick the three cards you are guided to pick.
Set the intention prior to shuffling that the top three cards of the deck will be the right cards for you. Once you have finished shuffling, pick the top three cards,

then lay them out as the top card being about your past, the middle card being about your present and the third card being about guidance for your future. Lay them out and then off you go, following the formula from above. Enjoy!

**The heart reading**

Lay your cards out in a heart shape then pick as many cards as you're guided to with the formula above. This is a great reading when you're needing or wanting extra TLC, (tender loving care). You deserve it.

**The chuck reading**

This can be a great reading to do when things have become a bit stressful and you've been too in your head and not switching off very well. It's recommended before this reading that you close your eyes, put some favourite or calming music on and light a candle or two. Take ten breaths in and out, sitting or lying down, tucked up in a cosy blanket. When it says 'chuck' it doesn't mean everywhere! Just gently 'chuck' them on the carpet or floor. Close your eyes and pick one to five cards that you are drawn to. Ask your guardian angel to help you pick the right cards in a clairsentient/feeling way.

**TIP!**

**Remember, always thank your guardian angel after the reading. Silently is fine; angels love gratitude.**

## How to pick angel cards or positive affirmation cards with friends and family

The best tip is to keep it simple. You don't need to introduce the angel prayer or meditation unless you're guided to! Ask (silently) your angels to ensure the reading is positive. It's not about explaining the rest of this book or your angels to them, it's about spending quality time with your friends, family, children and others during the good, challenging and sad times of life. Use the angel cards and positive affirmation cards to help you open up conversations, perhaps over a cup of tea or favourite drink, at dinner, or anytime you believe the cards will be of help.

### Here's a simple exercise to get you started:

⟩ Shuffle the cards.

⟩ Fan the cards out.

⟩ Ask your friends or family to pick a card and look at it and read it out loud.

⟩ Say to them: *What does the card message mean to you?*

⟩ Listen.

⟩ Then join in, talking about what they said and sharing in their experience.

⟩ Then swap over.

⟹ They shuffle the cards, and fan them out.

⟹ You pick your card and read it.

⟹ Then it's your turn to say what it means to you.

⟹ Then discuss together about your cards.

⟹ Talk to your angels and thank them for your guidance.


If you want to, pick another card together. However, although many cards feel right for you, often one card is perfect. You can enjoy this in person, as well as on Facetime, WhatsApp, Zoom, Skype, etc. How wonderful is that?

And finally.

Creating something visual together with your family or friends is a wonderful thing to do. Ask the angels for guidance and use your angel cards if that helps. As a group of friends or family, create your vision board with things each of you love about your relationship with each other as well as things you want to bring into your relationship in the future. It could be to have more children, or a holiday, decorating a room, spending time cooking together, planning and growing a garden, having a new hobby, or just creating time and space to be together. Put visual reminders on your board and share in your goals to achieve this. Thank the angels for their help and guidance.

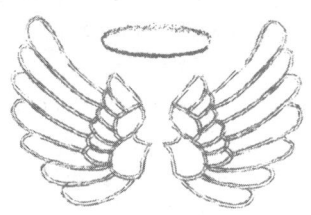

# Chapter 11

*"Be kind whenever possible.
It is always possible."*

**Dalai Lama**

## Communicating with children

This chapter isn't just for parents and carers of children, it is also for those of you who work with children in some way or who enjoy the company of your nieces, nephews, godchildren, children of friends or any child you meet. This will help you communicate with children, even if it's not a natural thing for you to do!

There are two words that summarise how to communicate best with children, and they are, are you ready? Drum roll. *Be friendly*. It's as simple as that. These words were given by a child, and well, it really is key isn't it? Children love to be spoken to in a friendly way. Have you noticed when you're moody, stressed or angry it makes those around you more stressed and upset? Have you noticed when a child's upset, moody, angry or anxious that when they speak to you in that way it can be easy to reply in that way? However, children don't respond well when someone else replies in that way. They will, however, respond well if you keep your tone of voice as calm and friendly as possible. Try it and you will most probably see them snap out of it much quicker. This will help you get to the bottom of what's really going on with them and how best to find resolutions to their problems, challenges and any sadness that they may be experiencing.

The skills you are going to learn in the chapter are not only for communicating with children; you are going to learn to communicate with your guardian angel at the same time. This will really add another dimension and can help you see things from a different perspective.

You can use some of the techniques we have covered in the book with children, and be reassured, they will love to do the exercises or play with the angel cards with you. Here are some ideas.

Start by asking your guardian angel simple questions at the beginning of the day or when you're with a child or children, giving yourself permission to receive the answers

You might say silently: *How shall I be with* ... (insert child's name(s) today?) Your guardian angel may say: 'friendly'.

Then expand on it. *How can I be friendly today?* Your guardian angel will give you clues. The words 'park' or 'park and coffee shop' or 'card game' or something similar might pop into your head.

The same applies if you are looking after a child who is in a bad mood or not responding to you.

Ask your guardian angel: *How shall I be with...* (insert their name(s))?

*How can I help them to be more happy?*

*What do you think would be good to do together today?*

*What can I do to communicate in a more friendly way with them?*

Sometimes, it's not the child that is feeling in a bad mood. Adults have bad moods too!

There is one magic trick or approach you can adopt with children when you're feeling annoyed, stressed or angry. Ideally the first thing to do is take some TIME OUT. Literally. Ideally find some time to be on your own for a while, if that is what is needed.

Most arguments with children, especially older children, often stem from the adult not having had enough sleep, or being stressed about money, being in a horrible relationship or some sadness or challenge that's going on that they can't switch off from. It might just be (if you are a lady) that it's the time of the month and experiencing some PMT symptoms of moodiness or that you are just tired. It's not easy caring for children!

Always remember, these things are not the child's fault. You need to find a way to put these things aside so you are kind, friendly and enjoy your child's company more.

The number 10 meditation is a great tool to use in these moments. You can teach it to children too.

**The number 10 meditation**

Take yourself into a private space if you can. If you have little ones, make sure they are well supervised.

Or you can still be in the same space with your children and they can do this with you.

This can be done extremely practically, either sitting, standing or lying down. You don't have to light a candle or do any preparation. When you need to, just get on with it!

Start by wiggling your body, loosening up your joints the best you can; shake out any tension and relax your shoulders, letting them drop down and know that deep in your heart and soul that your number 10 meditation is going to instantly make you feel better. Ask your guardian angel to be with you. Here we go:

*Take ten breaths in and out, breathing in through your nose and out through your mouth, relax.*

*Breathe in through your nose and out through your mouth, relax.*

*Breathe in through your nose and out through your mouth, relax.*

*Breathe in through your nose and out through your mouth, relax.*

*Breathe in through your nose and out through your mouth, relax.*

*Breathe in through your nose and out through your mouth, relax.*

*Breathe in through your nose and out through your mouth, relax.*

*Breathe in through your nose and out through your mouth, relax.*

*Breathe in through your nose and out through your mouth, relax.*

*Breathe in through your nose and out through your mouth, relax.*

Once you've enjoyed your ten breaths in and out, have a shake and wiggle and off you go again, thinking of positive and friendly ways you can be with your children on this day. You'll feel better knowing that you've taken some important time for you and knowing you'll enjoy the rest of your day more easily and effortlessly.

You can breathe and count out loud with your children. Make it fun and relaxing. It will calm you down and will certainly calm your children down too! It can be just the break you all need.

**TIP!** **You can do this in a less than a minute, so you *do* have time.**

Positive affirmations work wonders for you and your children. You can think them, say them out loud, write them, draw them, and share the experience however you like with children.

**TIP!** **There are cards designed especially for children. Try my Happy Kids Cards® They are great for parents, carers and primary school teachers.**

*I am happy and full of energy.*

*I am energetic. I radiate good energy wherever I go.*

*I love to smile. Smiling makes me happy.*

*I am happy. I feel happy inside and out.*

*I love to read. Reading makes me happy.*

*I stretch every day. I do a full body stretch every day. Lying on my back I stretch my arms and legs.*

*I am creative. I love to make things.*

*Getting lots of fresh air, walks and exercise makes me more fun and creative.*

*I enjoy exercise. I love to run around, swim or enjoy my favourite hobby.*

*I have a great imagination. I always have lots of good ideas.*

*I sing with happiness. Music makes me happy.*

*I dance with joy. Dancing is so much fun.*

*I think positive words. I find solutions.*

*I am honest. I am proud of myself. I like telling the truth.*

*I smile and laugh. I smile laugh and I play today.*

*I am funny; today I enjoy something fun.*

*I love to play. Playing makes me happy.*

*I visualise and see happiness. I love thinking of a favourite memory. I shut my eyes and remember. I am good at this.*

*I am healthy. Healthy foods, drink and water make me feel good.*

*I am loved. I am surrounded by love.*

*I have a lovely family. I love spending time with family I love and trust.*

*I am strong. I keep myself fit and strong every day.*

*I am kind. I treat others as I expect to be treated myself.*

*Well done, I did really well at something today.*

*Thank you. I am grateful for... (fill in the blanks) and happy about today.*

*I have strong tummy muscles. I love doing some exercise and having strong tummy muscles.*

*I love to practice. I have worked really hard.*

*I have lovely friends. I enjoy spending fun time with my friends.*

*I make a wish. I let my wish fly in the sky in a red balloon filled with love.*

*What I like about me is.......... (fill in the blank).*

*I am fun. I love to do fun things.*

*I love setting goals. I love to think, write or draw my goals. (Picture what I want to create).*

*I am patient. I easily wait my turn.*

*I am a good listener. I listen well.*

*I love to learn. What did I learn today?*

*My life is magic. I think of one way my life is magic right now.*

*I concentrate well. I focus and concentrate well.*

*I have good posture. When I sit and stand tall, I feel happy and my back feels stronger.*

*I am a wonderful person. I am confident.*

*I breathe and relax. I breathe in through my nose into my tummy, like a balloon inflating. I breathe out through my mouth and relax.*

*I am calm, I can stay calm.*

*I ask for help. I ask those I trust and love for help.*

*I am quiet. I shut my eyes, breathe in through my nose, breathe out through my mouth and relax.*

*I lie down to relax. I lie on my back, knees bent, arms at shoulder height and relax.*

*I love to slow down. I take a break and rest to recharge my batteries.*

*My muscles are relaxed. I love having a bath or shower to relax my muscles.*

*I am relaxed. I relax before bedtime.*

*I am peaceful. All is calm and well, I am at peace within.*

*I sleep well. I love going to bed and getting plenty of sleep for me.*

## Journal with your children and your guardian angel about these positive affirmations

In your angel journal, write down how the affirmations made you and the children feel.

Ask your guardian angel: *Are there any other messages you'd like to give me about my day?* Write down what comes to you from your angel. Keep a note of all the positive things about your day and what else you can do to make every day as much fun.

## Journal with your guardian angel using your angel cards

You can try this when your children are sleeping in the evening or napping during the day or out at school.

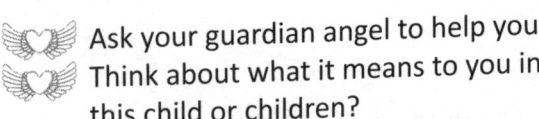 Ask your guardian angel to help you pick a card. Think about what it means to you in relation to this child or children?

In your angel journal, write down what it means to you.

Ask your guardian angel, *Are there any other*

*messages you'd like to give me about this affirmation and message in relation to this child or children?* Write down what comes to you from your guardian angel.

**TIP!**

**You can speak directly to their guardian angel too. Make it clear who you're communicating with.**

### How to use angel cards with your children

It's a wonderful thing to bring the angel cards into children's lives. They can be used in the same way as the positive affirmations. You might like to add in that we each have a guardian angel and tell them they can ask their guardian angel to help them pick a card or that they can pick a card with their guardian angel and teddy. For older children at secondary school age it's wonderful for them to have their own decks of cards too – they like to choose how they pick them. You can show them the way; it's easy. It's a brilliant thing to do together regularly but also something that you may both like to do to help in every area of your lives and in your own private space too.

The easiest way to get children to start using the cards is to pick a card every single day to start the day, end the day, or at bedtime. For teachers, pick a card in class or whenever something is stressful, sad or a challenge has cropped up or if you simply want to feel happier. For children, we want it to be fun and to keep it simple.

**First time exercise using the cards with children**

1. Shuffle or mix up the cards.
2. Either fan out the cards or spread them on your bed, table or floor face down.
3. Ask your child to pick the card you like the look of the most.
4. They can pick another card if you want to; you might like to pick as many three.

Read the cards, say them out loud, and think about and talk together about what they mean to you all.

**Here are four more fun places where you can pick positive affirmation, Happy Kids Cards® or angel cards with children:**

1. In the car on a long journey. You can ask the children to pick and read them out.
2. At breakfast time surprise your children and dish up the Happy Kids Cards® or angel cards in a cereal bowl!
3. Let them take them to Nanny and Grandad's or on holiday. They will enjoy sharing what they have learnt with others.
4. Show their friends on a play date, sleepover or party.

**Here are six more fun ideas for children to use positive affirmation, Happy Kids Cards® or angel cards**

1. Make a happy face with them.
2. Get a favourite soft toy to pick the card.
3. Make the cards into the initial letter of your name, such as J for John, M for Maya.
4. Make a heart shape.
5. Make a rainbow, star, circle, square, or triangle shape.
6. Make up your own creative way of using the Happy Kids Cards®, positive affirmation cards or angel cards.

**For older children from secondary school age, it can be brilliant to use this approach**

It's a good activity to take you away from mobile phones and electronic devices! Make it a rule that you leave these in another room when practising this activity.

1. Shuffle or mix up the cards.
2. Either fan out the cards or spread them on your bed, table or floor face down.
3. Ask your guardian angel to help you pick the card you like the look of the most (you can do this silently).
4. Pick another card if you want to; you might like to pick even as many as three cards.
5. Read the card, say it out loud, and think or talk about what it means to you.
6. Swap over and let the other person pick the card and talk about it next. Both of you having a turn is useful and for a shy child be prepared to go

first to show them how it's done. It's a good way to open up conversations with a teenager and get them to talk to you!

**TIP!**

**If your child found certain cards more inspiring, dot these around the house for them to find. Even just knowing that this tool is at hand is a wonderful thing. When there are stressful moments such as starting a new school always have them at hand or make them visible.**

Here are some other ways to have fun with your children. And you may be surprised to hear that we are going to look at good posture! The angels encourage us to have good posture too.

### How good posture can bring more harmony to children and you

"What is good posture?" says a 10-year-old child who's never heard of this word. You can say, *Well, if you slouch, this is bad posture*, and you can demonstrate by slouching whether you're sitting or standing. Then stand up tall or sit tall with good posture with your back straight (the ideal way is with the natural curves of the spine).

Stand with your feet hip width apart, arms relaxed by your side with your eyes forward. It's like you have helium balloons attached to the top of your head, lengthening your spine up towards the sky.

A simple demonstration of this is being able to walk around a room with a soft toy on top of your head – this is the perfect version to show younger children and primary school age children. Secondary school children, although they may still love soft toys usually prefer to balance a book on top of their head and walk around the room. See how they will rise to this challenge and have a go!

When we feel moody, stressed, unhappy or nervous, we rarely sit or stand with good posture. Whereas when we feel confident, happy or ecstatic, say, after winning a race at athletics, we stand tall and our posture improves. This is good for the spine, body, muscles, back and neck but also has a huge impact on your confidence and happiness. You can find out a lot more about this and the science behind it in Dr David Hamilton's book *I Heart Me: The Science of Self-Love* as well as the TED Talk by Harvard University Psychologist Amy Cuddy: *Your body language may shape who you are.* It's absolutely fascinating stuff that you can fake it till you make it with your body language, although as Amy says in her TED talk, "fake it till you become it" and clearly she's meaning to practice.

The *I am enough power pose* which Amy finishes her TED talk with is so much fun. Try it for yourself in times of stress. Whatever the situation, she says, you can go to the bathroom or somewhere private and do the power pose.

**Power pose as recommended by Amy Cuddy**

Simply stand with good posture for two minutes or even adopt the power pose – see below. Try it. Time yourself to hold this pose for two minutes. Smile and release from the pose and then off you go. How does this make you feel?

**A fun way to do the I am enough power pose is with music and on the spot dancing!**

Time yourself to allow two minutes.

- ♡ Stand with really good posture. Stand with your feet hip width apart, arms relaxed by your side with your eyes forward and imagine you have helium balloons attached to the top of your head, lengthening your spine up towards the sky.
- ♡ Or stand as above with your hands on your hips!
- ♡ Put a great song on and enjoy the power pose for the entire song or for at least the two minutes.
- ♡ Whilst you are standing there, either keep thinking, "I am enough", say out loud, *I am enough* or sing to the tune of your favourite song to the words *I am enough*, and smile.
- ♡ You can look in the mirror at the same time too or just do it.
- ♡ As well as standing in your power pose, at the same time you can bop or dance and move around on the spot with this good posture, whilst you smile and say *I am enough.*

How do you feel after? Bet you feel better!
This is a great exercise to do with your children and doing anything with them that you all enjoy will certainly strengthen your bond with them and help you create the harmonious relationships you desire. Here's another one for you to try.

- Standing with your feet hip width apart, standing tall and with good posture, look forward.
- Place your hands on your hips. Say, *I am enough*.
- Place your hands just behind your neck or at the side of your neck if that's more comfortable for you, squeeze your elbows back a little bit if comfortable and say, *I am enough.*
- Place your arms in the air, feeling really happy, and say, *I am enough*.
- Repeat this sequence five times or for up to two minutes, and smile.

Journal with your guardian angel about the relationships you have with your children and how what you have discovered in this chapter can improve this.
Make your plan of action for how you can build in more time and better relationships with your children.

**Journal with your angel**

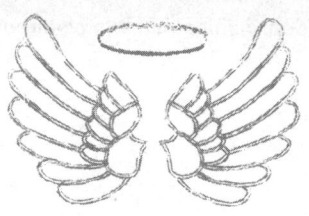

## Chapter 12

*"We shall find peace.*
*We shall hear angels,*
*we shall see the sky sparkling with diamonds."*
**Anton Chekhov**

**Visualisation and manifestation**

The angels are very excited to talk about how visualisation can bring more of what you want into your life. Visualisation is often thought of as being able to see or 'visualise' something in your mind. A lot of people think that they can't visualise, but you can, in your own unique way – and the angels will show you how if you feel like this. The power of the mind is a fascinating thing, and if you're needing or wanting to manifest more of what you want in your life then this activity will be a brilliant tool. The Oxford Dictionary definition of visualisation is 'the representation of an object, situation, or set of information as a chart or other image.'

The exciting thing is you can use the power of meditation, practicing what you want in both your mind and through physical practice too. Sports scientists and sports psychologists are well known for helping top sports men and women excel and improve at their given sport with the power of a positive mindset and visualisation. However, for example, a professional golfer wouldn't just practice in their mind and expect to play brilliantly on the course.

Inviting your guardian angel into your visualisation and manifestation journey is a truly wonderful thing. By working with your guardian angel in meditation then spending time writing about what you visualised and experienced, as well as making notes and plans about how you can make these things happen, you will soon see your dreams unfold. You'll think to yourself, "I dreamed that, I saw that coming, I made it happen". It's because you put in the work and took the guidance from your guardian angel.

Think about:

 What do you want to create and bring into your life?

 What would you love to manifest into your work or business?

Did you know, according to Dr David Hamilton PhD, neuroscience research shows that the brain doesn't distinguish what is real from what is imaginary'?

So, the more you can think about what you want to create, the easier it is to bring it into reality. It's exciting to know and worth getting your head around as it may be one of the best gifts you give yourself in your life.

You can use it anywhere and anytime so long as it's a positive thing. The angels will help you with your manifestation at a deeper level.

Here's another interesting fact from Dr David Hamilton: It takes 21 to 66 days to wire a new good habit into the brain, so it takes consistent practice to make this happen. In part one of this book we looked at the importance of practice. Here's the evidence that confirms this.

Have you noticed some things come more naturally to you than others? When you dig a little deeper you'll find that you will have practiced whatever that thing is many times to get to the stage you're at, rewiring your brain in the process.

Let's look at some exercises we can do to help, starting with turning our negatives into positives.

**Turn what feels wrong to what you want in your life**

Say your angel prayer:

*Guardian angel, please surround me with your unconditional love; shine your bright light on me for guidance, for positivity, healing, happiness and inspiration. Let your light shine on me like the sun, in my life and my work. Guardian angel, please help me to talk to you and to receive your guidance and love to fill my life with positive actions.*
*With gratitude, I thank you.*

Close your eyes and take five relaxing breaths in and out, breathing in through your nose and out through your nose, relaxing more and more on each out breath.

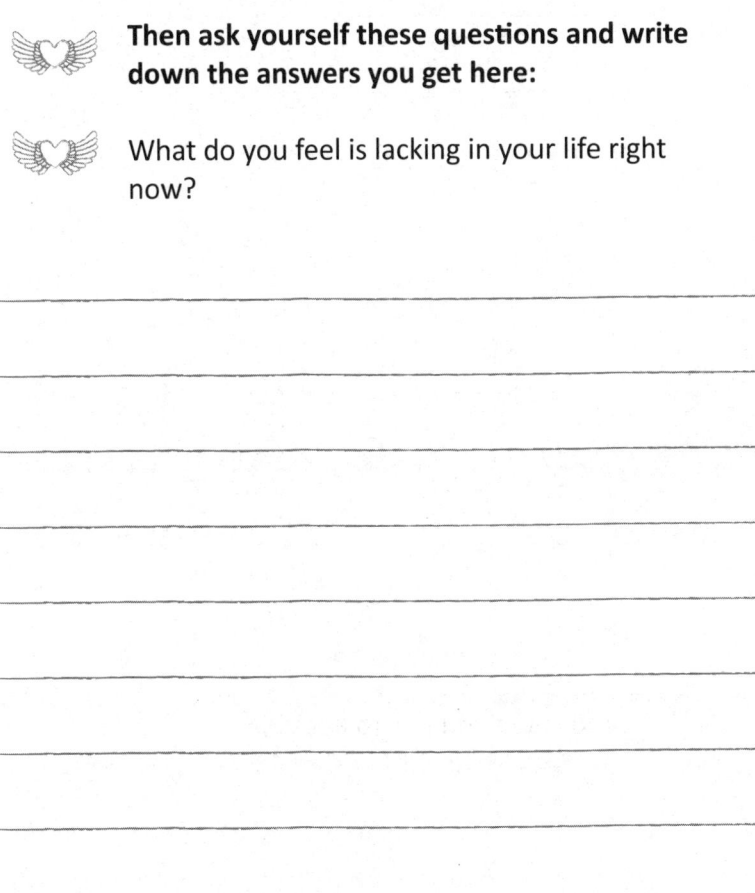

**Then ask yourself these questions and write down the answers you get here:**

What do you feel is lacking in your life right now?

_____

_____

_____

_____

_____

_____

_____

_____

_____

_____

What is wrong? What can you do about it?

_____

_____

_____

_____

_____

_____

_____

_____

_____

_____

_____

Who could you talk to about it?

_____

_____

_____

_____

What would make this right?

_____

_____

_____

_____

_____

_____

_____

_____

_____

Write down what you want to happen instead of what's going wrong. Write your inspirations and thoughts down here:

_____

_____

_____

 Then ask your guardian angel for solutions.

**Ask your guardian angel to help you write down ideas to help the new goal become a reality.**

Take any divinely guided action steps. Write them down in your angel journal.

When you have done this go on a walk or try an angel meditation to speed up your manifestation and to bring it into fruition.

Sit with your guardian angel and journal together afterwards.
This is very similar to the above exercise, except this time you're ready and inspired to only focus on what you're wanting to manifest. Hooray for this!

*"Today is your day.*
*Your mountain is waiting so get on your way."*
**Dr Seuss**

**Manifest your desires with the angels exercise**

Say your angel prayer:

*Guardian angel, please surround me with your
unconditional love; shine your bright light on me for
guidance, for positivity, healing, happiness and
inspiration. Let your light shine on me like the sun, in
my life and my work. Guardian angel, please help me
to talk to you and to receive your guidance and love
to make positive changes in my life.*
*With gratitude, I thank you.*

- Close your eyes and take five relaxing breaths in and out, breathing in through your nose and out through your nose, relaxing more and more on each out breath.
- Then ask yourself this question:
- What do you want to happen in your life?
- Write down what answers you get here or in your angel journal.
- Write your aspirations and thoughts down.
- Ask your guardian angel to help you write down ideas to help the new goal to become a reality. Take any divinely guided action steps. Write them down here.

Once you have done this, go on a walk or enjoy the manifestation with the angels meditation on page 208.

Always thank your guardian angel each time they help or inspire you.

**Positive affirmations**

**Here are some affirmations for you to say to yourself or out loud to help guide you with your angels:**

*I create my own reality.*

*I love manifesting my hearts desires.*

*I am good at visualisation.*

*Practice makes for improvement.*

*I love to practice; I love to see myself improving.*

*Meditation is my best friend.*

*Manifestation is my best friend.*

*Visualisation is my best friend.*

*Visualising my goals makes them come true.*

*I focus on what I want.*

*I enjoy the journey, each and every moment.*

*Thank you for bringing my hopes and dreams into reality.*

*Thank you for the joy in my manifestation with the angels.*

*I am grateful for.............. (fill in the blank of what you want to manifest). Thank you, angels.*

*I love to smile.*

*I love to talk to my angels.*

**Meditation**

This meditation is designed to help you visualise what you're wanting to bring into your life with a visualisation of your desires, remembering that your brain doesn't understand the difference between what's real and what's not! Your guardian angel will give you extra guidance during the meditation as you want to allow your goals and dreams to expand to their full potential. They may have something even better in store for you. Your guardian angel will guide the way. Talk to them and ask for their help.

## Manifestation with the angels meditation

> Close your eyes and relax, sitting or lying down. You might like to tuck yourself up in a cosy soft blanket with a cushion behind your head. Have your knees bent if you want some more back support, feet hip width apart or legs straight if that's comfortable for you.

Say your angel prayer:

*Guardian angel, please surround me with your unconditional love; shine your bright light on me for guidance, for positivity, healing, happiness and inspiration. Let your light shine on me like the sun, in my life and my work. Guardian angel, please help me to talk to you and to receive your guidance and love to visualise what I need in my life right now.*
*With gratitude, I thank you.*

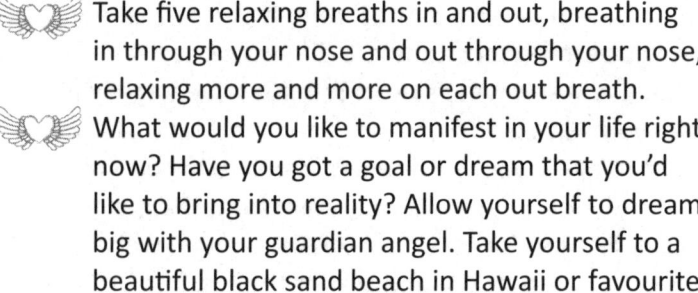

Take five relaxing breaths in and out, breathing in through your nose and out through your nose, relaxing more and more on each out breath.

What would you like to manifest in your life right now? Have you got a goal or dream that you'd like to bring into reality? Allow yourself to dream big with your guardian angel. Take yourself to a beautiful black sand beach in Hawaii or favourite

beach; a turtle is waiting there to greet you for
you to take you on a retreat especially for you,
your health, well-being and whole life, for your
mind, body and spirit. It's a sanctuary created
especially for you and it's magically turned into a
private beach. You feel in love with this time you
have for yourself to both recharge your batteries
and to visualise what you're wanting to bring
into your life. Now, you're going to allow it to
become real in your mind.

 Ask your guardian angel to help make it real
through visions, or hearing messages about this
coming true – it might be an inspirational song
with the lyrics or words that you need to hear
right now to help bring that goal into fruition.

 You may get a feeling of how your life will
become when this vision becomes a reality,
that feeling of joy in your heart and soul that
this has really shown up especially for you. You
may like to make yourself at home and sit in
a favourite stripy deckchair or a deckchair or
sun lounger of your choice; perhaps you fancy
sitting in one of those giant egg chairs with a
comfy mattress on it, or a swinging chair. There's
even an amethyst beach hut there for you if you
fancy some healing inspiration from the deep
vibrant, glistening crystal that shimmers in the
light, every shade of purple you can imagine.
You can sit or lie outside with the sounds of the
waves lapping on the shore. The sea is pretty
calm; as your breathing calms the sea becomes
calmer too. As your breathing becomes calmer,

the wind and breeze calm in the summer air. The temperature is perfect for you and you enjoy having not a care in the world, not having to be anywhere or do anything.

You know deep in your soul this is your place to *be*, it's like a sanctuary especially for you. In the distance you have a sense that there are dolphins having fun and squeaking with delight playing in the water. Their goal that day is to play and be joyful, have fun and have a smooth, flowing journey ahead of them, to be kind and compassionate to all and send love to you and the entire planet.

You see your guardian angel sit or lie down next to you, and you have that strong sense that their wings have wrapped around you, filling you with a sense of support and guidance every step of the way. They are cheering you on that you want more for your life and they are there for you to guide you.

Allow yourself to know your guardian angel is with you. You may see your guardian angel vividly in their colours, aura or actually see them in your mind's eye. Be in awe as you allow this vision to appear – alternatively, give your guardian angel permission to float words into your mind for guidance. It's like you have a typewriter in your head. It's so useful!

Breathing in through your nose, as you exhale through your mouth, relax. Now you see these rose quartz heart shaped crystals embedded on the beach hut and as you glance at them you realise your guardian angel got you to open your eyes just for a moment to notice that loving sign just for you.

And relax; close your eyes.

Breathing in through your nose, exhale through your nose and relax.

Allow your goal or dream to float more and more vividly into your mind's eye, knowing what it's like for it to come true. Allow yourself to daydream with your guardian angel. Ask aloud, *guardian angel, what personal messages would you like me to receive about this manifestation coming true?*

Your guardian angel hands you a gift of a message especially for you. It's gift wrapped in an angel box which is wrapped in wrapping paper that looks just like your guardian angel, with a bow wrapped around in your favourite colour. You open it and it's really clear as you open it what your gift of guidance is.

Your guardian angel hands you another gift of guidance. You open the box, which glitters like an amethyst crystal with a purple bow. You open it and receive another gift of guidance about your manifestation from your guardian angel. You give thanks.

Your guardian angel hands you another gift of guidance. You open the box – this box is all the colours of the rainbow and makes you smile. It has a bright yellow ribbon and bow. You open it and receive another gift of guidance about your manifestation from your guardian angel. You say thank you.

Your guardian angel hands you a final gift of guidance. You open the box – this box is a giant box and has a picture of your manifestation on it on the wrapping paper. You are astonished and happy. The ribbon is every colour under the rainbow. You open it and receive another gift of guidance about your manifestation from your guardian angel. You give thanks.

You're excited to have received all of these gifts and as you daydream about what it is you want to manifest, you realise that if you decide to you can just twizzle round where you are and you'll be able to vividly see another benefit of your manifestation coming true. What else will it mean? How else will this coming true enhance both your life and the lives of others? You see so many different positive situations and opportunities coming to you. It's a joy to just soak up the positivity of this meditation.

You remember that practice makes for improvement and that you can give yourself this gift of manifestation meditation with your guardian angel whenever you like. You may feel your guardian angel tickle your head or face to let you know their presence is real; that they are there for you unconditionally.

If you're guided to, walk slowly to the water's edge and gaze at the beauty of the sun rising early in the morning, it's so beautiful and energising and as you see the sun appear on the horizon, you give thanks to the angels and universe for your manifestation coming true. You picture a red balloon and allow this balloon to float off into the sky with the gratitude of your dream and goal already having manifested. You saw it, you believed it, you created it. Allow yourself to receive this visualisation often in meditation to enable the neuroplasticity of your brain to rewire to make more and more aspects of your manifestation real. You deserve this. The planet deserves this. Your loved ones deserve this. You are deserving and much loved by the angels.

Take a deep breath in and out or yawn. Wiggle your fingers and toes. On the Hawaiian beach, take a paddle and get a beautiful glass of water with sliced lemon in! It's delicious. Your guardian angel smiles at you, and thanks you for your time together as you thank them too. She places a beautiful Hawaiian flower lei round your neck and the smell of the flowers is incredible and anchors you into this happy memory any time you like. The flowers are a deep cerise pink and you dance with joy at the serenity, peace and happiness you feel right now.

You take a deep breath in of the Hawaiian sea air, you exhale and relax, you take another breath of Hawaiian sea air and you jump for joy with gratitude. Thank you, angels.

Open your eyes. Take a drink of water, open a window, perhaps enjoy a cup of tea and take some time to sit down and write down everything you remember from this meditation.

> What ideas came to you? What did you see, feel?
>
> Are there any steps you can take to put these ideas into action?

It helps to keep these in mind by daydreaming about them.

**Here's a short exercise you can do every day to help you stay on track:**

Write down a goal, however big or small, that you would like to achieve

I would like to achieve

_____

_____

_____

_____

_____

_____

And then close your eyes, breathe and relax.

Daydream about your goal coming true. See the colours, hear the sounds, experience how it feels when you see yourself in your daydream achieving these goals. Talk to your guardian angel and ask them to daydream with you. Ask for their help and guidance to see the colours, the sounds and the feelings. Do this for as long as feels good for you.

Afterwards, simply take a few moments writing down what inspiration and guidance came to you.

## Journal with your angel

I Talk to Angels

And to end this beautiful journey your I Talk to Angels book should now be full of your notes and doodles and everything you have shared with your angels - your thoughts, hopes, plans and dreams.

Hold your book in both hands close to your heart and close your eyes, remembering everything about this wonderful journey and say:

*I thank you angels for sharing my journey through this book with me.*

*All is OK in my life as I know I have you by my side.*

*I trust you, my angels.*

*I trust myself.*

*I talk to my angels.*

*They talk to me too.*

*I love my angels.*

*My angels love me too, always.*

*I Talk to Angels.*

*"Wheresoever you go, go with all your heart."*
**Confucious**

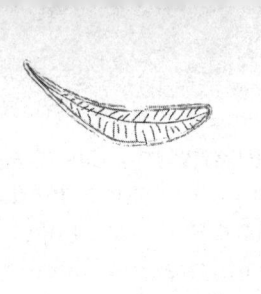

# Acknowledgements

My sincere thanks goes to Janey Lee Grace for encouraging me to write this book and supporting me to make it happen, my publisher Caroline Peden Smith for believing in me and working with me to produce a book that I am so very proud of and my designer Lara Peralta who has produced the beautiful illustrations and design.

I would also like to thank my wonderful family, Mum, Dad, sister Julie, son Sammy and my friends for their love and support. I would especially like to thank Dame Kelly Holmes for sharing her love of the angels with us and for her inspiration to help us follow our dreams

Lastly, I would like to thank my guardian angel for always being there to guide me. You are so precious to me.

# About the author

**Beverley Densham** is an Angel expert. She graduated from the University of Brighton with a degree in Sports Science and became a Pilates expert. A near death experience guided her to change direction. Studying with Doreen Virtue®, she became a certified Angel Therapy® Practitioner and now inspires others and runs Angelversity, an Angel and Reiki healing practitioner course with her company Angelic Lifestyle.

To find out more or to get in touch with Beverley, visit:
Website: www.angeliclifestyle.com
Twitter @BeverleyDensham
Instagram: beverleydensham
Facebook @beverleymdensham

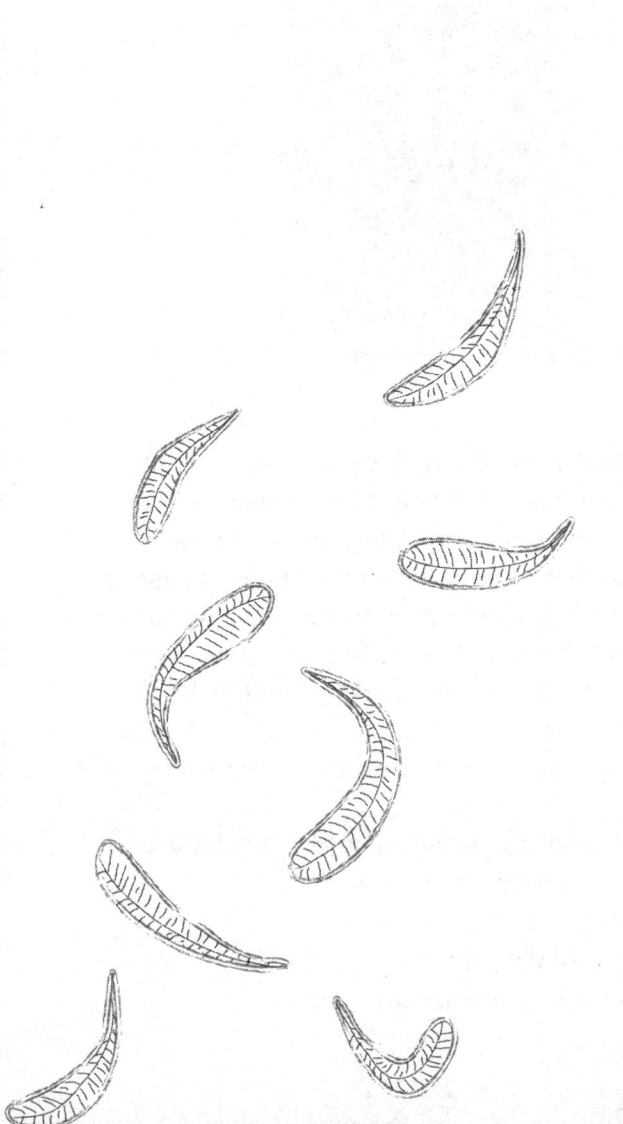